Robert G. Ingersoll
A Checklist

THE SERIF SERIES: BIBLIOGRAPHIES AND CHECKLISTS

GENERAL EDITOR: William White, Wayne State University

Robert G. Ingersoll

A Checklist

By Gordon Stein

Ohio State University

The Kent State University Press

"America don't know how proud
she ought to be of Ingersoll"
—Walt Whitman

The Serif Series: Number 9
Bibliographies and Checklists

William White, General Editor
Wayne State University

Copyright © 1969 by Gordon Stein
All rights reserved
Library of Congress Catalogue Number 78-626234
Standard Book Number 87338-047-9
Manufactured in the United States of America at the
press of The Oberlin Printing Company
Designed by Merald E. Wrolstad

First Edition

TO:
MJB who encouraged me
and to
SAT who put up with it

Acknowledgements

Perhaps one reason why no one has ever compiled an Ingersoll checklist or bibliography before is because the job is so difficult. Many of the items are not found in the usual collections, and others have virtually disappeared. My thanks are therefore extended to the many people who made my job easier.

This book would not have been possible without the help of the following people: Professor Matthew J. Bruccoli of Ohio State University, who first aroused my interest in bibliography; Miss Jane Gatliff and Mr. Richard Gray of the OSU Library; Sherman Day Wakefield, Frank Swancara, Nathan Simons, Jack Benjamin, Kit Mouat, J. S. L. Gilmour, David Collis and Joseph Lewis for advice, books and sympathy. Finally, I would like to thank the staff of the Kent State University Press for their help and interest in seeing the checklist published.

Contents

Introduction

Robert Green Ingersoll (1833-1899) was one of the giants
of the nineteenth century. The son of a Protestant minister,
he started as a school teacher, read law, and soon became well
known as a lawyer in Shawneetown and then Peoria, Illinois.
His oratorical prowess soon brought requests for him to speak.
Ingersoll's integrity would allow him to say only what he
believed to be true. He could not be a hypocrite. He would
talk about the failings of "Christianity" as readily as about
Shakespeare. Although Ingersoll did give a few addresses
before the Civil War, it was after he returned as a Colonel
that he began to devote a large amount of his time to
public lectures.

He had been appointed Attorney General of Illinois, but
his reputation remained a regional one. Ingersoll was offered
the Republican nomination for Governor of Illinois if he would
keep his religious views to himself; he refused as a matter of
principle.

In 1876 Ingersoll first came to national attention when
he nominated James G. Blaine for the presidency at the
Republican Convention at Cincinnati. This was the famous
"Plumed Knight" speech, an epithet which Blaine carried
from then on.

The Ingersoll family moved to Washington, D. C. where
Ingersoll's reputation as a lawyer continued to grow. He received

much publicity for his successful defense in the Star Route Case, which involved millions of dollars supposedly defrauded by his clients from the Post Office Department.

Ingersoll's lecturing schedule grew along with his fame. He was drawing standing-room-only crowds of over three thousand people in every major city of the country in the 1880's. His large lecture fees (about two thousand dollars per night based on a percentage of the "house") plus his law practice brought him an annual income of over one hundred thousand dollars. However, most of this was given away to charities and to needy people. As a result of his generosity, he died a comparatively poor man.

Ingersoll died peacefully in bed from a sudden heart attack in his sixty-sixth year. Contrary to some stories still in circulation, he never recanted nor regretted his actions.

An evaluation of the effect of Ingersoll's work in a historical context is difficult. To some extent, he performed the work of "Darwin's Bulldog" in the United States by helping the Theory of Evolution to gain acceptance. He was often accused by ministers of attacking religious ideas of a type which no one currently believed in. However, this does not seem to be the case when account is taken of the era in which he lived. During the period from 1850 to 1900 one of the bitterest battles between science and religion took place. It was the deciding point in the acceptance of the modern idea of the value and potential of science as a revealer of facts about the universe. It marked the beginnings of our modern outlook on the world. Ingersoll was not an innovator of the new ideas, but he was a popularizer of them. He served as a vehicle for bringing more of these new ideas to the American people than probably any other man. For this he has earned a niche in history.

Robert Ingersoll had a standard series of lectures. He would go on tour delivering two or three different ones per

tour. Each year he would add one or two new ones. Most of his
lectures were given without the use of notes, although they
were by no means "extemporaneous." Most of the standard
lectures were written down at first, memorized, and then
expanded or condensed during subsequent deliveries. One of
the most difficult problems in Ingersoll bibliography is the
existence of several versions of similar lectures with the same
title. Many vary in length and in content but contain some
identical sections.

Ingersoll's brother-in-law, C. P. Farrell, of Peoria, then
Washington, D. C., then New York City, was his authorized
publisher. Farrell published versions of Ingersoll's lectures
which were often largely rewritten and revised from the spoken
form by Ingersoll. The final, i.e., most highly polished and
revised, form of each one of the standard lectures was published
by Farrell as part of the twelve-volume "Dresden Edition"
of Ingersoll's Collected Works after Ingersoll's death in 1899.

However, as Ingersoll went around the country lecturing,
many unethical publishers issued unauthorized versions of his
lectures. Usually these were taken from newspaper accounts of
the lectures, which in turn were compiled by having shorthand
reporters record the entire lecture. Of course, Ingersoll did
not receive any royalties from these publications. What is
more serious for the bibliographer, however, is the fact that
no two lectures were ever delivered in exactly the same manner.
Hence, the unauthorized versions of some of the lectures only
vaguely resemble the final, revised versions found in the
"Dresden Edition."

Often the titles were also changed, especially in the versions
published in England (also unauthorized). Sometimes the
title was changed to encourage public interest and sales, as
is the case with the title change in the English version of
"About Farming in Illinois" to "Farming in America."

Other examples are "Law, Not God" for one of the English
titles of "Humboldt;" "Is All of the Bible Inspired?" for
the third part of "The Christian Religion;" and "The Spirit of
the Age" for Ingersoll's preface to "Modern Thinkers."
Occasionally the title was changed by the publisher in order
deliberately to deceive the public into thinking that this was
a lecture they had not seen before. This type of change prompted
Ingersoll to issue the statement often found appended to the
last page in C. P. Farrell's authorized editions of the lectures.
The statement says:

> Washington, D. C., July 10, 1889
>
> I wish to notify the public that all books and pamphlets
> purporting to contain my lectures, and not containing the imprint
> of Mr. C. P. Farrell as publisher, are spurious, grossly inaccurate,
> filled with mistakes, horribly printed, and outrageously unjust
> to me. The publishers of all such are simply literary thieves
> and pirates, and are obtaining money from the public under
> false pretences. These wretches have published one lecture
> under four titles, and several others under two or three.
> I take this course to warn the public that these publications are
> fraudulent; the only correct editions being those published
> by Mr. C. P. Farrell.
>
> R. G. Ingersoll

Because Ingersoll's lectures were published with different
titles and varying contents, a great number of difficulties
arise in the classification and even identification of the contents
of the lectures. Hence the presence of a complete title index
in this checklist.

There are several other serious problems in Ingersoll
bibliography. The first of these is the fact that many publishers
failed to identify themselves or indicate the location or date
of their publications. This was probably done in fear
of reprisal by their friends and neighbors, since it was very

unacceptable to be an "infidel." This bibliographical problem is similar to, though not as troublesome as, the problem faced by bibliographers of erotica.

Another problem in Ingersoll bibliography is that a large percentage of the pamphlets and some of the books containing Ingersoll's writings were published by "fly-by-night" publishers, or by small, short-lived firms. This means that most were not listed in the standard *Publisher's Trade Lists* or in such things as *Books-in-Print*. Also, many libraries failed to collect these items or threw them out. There was evidently some question in the minds of many librarians at the time about the "respectability" of Ingersoll's writings. All this makes it difficult to locate copies of many of the works. For example, the author was unable to find a single copy of any of the twenty or so titles of Ingersoll's writings which were published by "Banner of Light." This problem has been largely overcome, however, by the foresight of the New York Public Library, the British Museum, and the Library of Congress in preserving these items, as well as by the kindness and generosity of many private collectors. Their help is acknowledged elsewhere in this checklist.

Additional problems are the "frighteningly complicated," to use J. S. L. Gilmour's[1] term, interrelationships between some of the publishers involved. C. P. Farrell was Ingersoll's brother-in-law and authorized publisher; however, he had no printing facilities of his own, so all of his later publications (i.e., after 1880) were printed by the Peter Eckler Press in New York. Through some sort of agreement, Peter Eckler also issued many of the Ingersoll publications under his own imprint. These were, as would be expected, printed from the same plates as the C. P. Farrell editions, with new title pages.

[1] J. S. L. Gilmour, "A Freethought Collection and its Predecessors," *The Book Collector* 11:184-196 (1962).

There was also an extreme degree of economy in the use of these plates. The C. P. Farrell publications were reissued many times over the years. Some are dated as early as 1874, and some as late as 1922. After this date, the C. P. Farrell Company was absorbed into the Truth Seeker Company of New York. The first year of publication is indicated by the copyright date on the back of the title page, but apparently there were virtually no changes in the text. In most cases, the identical plates were used on later editions. The only exception to this was that after 1900, when the twelve-volume Dresden Edition was first published, individual lectures were reissued using the plates of the Dresden Edition, including the page numbers in most cases.

Before the Dresden Edition plates were made, C. P. Farrell used the plates from the collected lectures he had published (i.e., *The Gods and Other Lectures* and *The Ghosts and Other Lectures*) for printing the separately issued titles which were included in the two books just mentioned. Page numbers were usually not changed from the originals. The binding color of many of the early C. P. Farrell publications varies tremendously. I have not been able to detect any pattern or significance to this variation; therefore, it has not been mentioned as a factor of importance in dating the various publications.

Some later editions published by entirely different companies (e.g. Freethought Press Association, New York) also used the plates of the Dresden Edition. In addition, the Truth Seeker Company often was the first to print a new Ingersoll lecture in the pages of its journal, the *Truth Seeker*. The type was then divided into page-length sections and used to produce a pamphlet with the Truth Seeker Company imprint on it.

The problem of interrelated publishing companies becomes even more complex when dealing with the English companies.

It seems that Annie Besant and Charles Bradlaugh
established the Freethought Publishing Company in London,
(no relation to the Freethought Publishing Company of
New York). G. W. Foote founded the Progressive Publishing
Company. R. Forder was associated with this company,
probably as the actual printer; some publications bear only
the Forder imprint, however. After Foote's death, the
G. W. Foote & Company, which was the descendant of the
Progressive Publishing Company, adopted the publishing
name of "Pioneer Press." Abel Heywood and Sons were the
publishers of "Leek Bijou Freethought Reprints." Some of
Heywood's publications were sold through a series of
booksellers, whose names appear on the cover of some of his
publications as part of the multiple imprint.

Because of their relatively minor importance to Ingersoll
bibliography, the following types of items have not been
included in this checklist:

1) Books on oratory, public speaking, eloquence, or anthologies
   of famous speeches which include only a speech or two
   by Ingersoll. There are literally hundreds of these,
   and they are of only peripheral interest to Ingersoll
   bibliography. No speeches made their first appearance in
   print in these anthologies.

2) Newspaper articles about Ingersoll's lectures or about
   Ingersoll. Over one hundred of the scrapbooks compiled
   by the Ingersoll family are now in the Library of Congress.
   Each scrapbook is packed solidly with newspaper
   clippings about Ingersoll. However, there are far too
   many, and they have too little identification as to origin, to
   be of much use.

3) Newspaper interviews with Ingersoll *unless* reprinted in
   Freethought periodicals of the time, which was often
   the case, especially with the more important interviews.

4) Periodical articles by Ingersoll which were published
   after 1900 (i.e., posthumously). These were just
   reprints of earlier articles or publications, often from the
   Dresden Edition. Some periodicals of this period (after
   1900) which *did* contain Ingersoll articles of this
   type were:
   Boston Investigator
   Common Sense which later became *The Freethinker*, then
       The Age of Reason (New York)
   The Freethinker (London)
   Humanitarian Review (Chicago)
   The Ingersoll Memorial Beacon (Chicago)
   Progressive World (Clifton, N. J., and later Los Angeles)
   Secular Thought (Toronto)
   The Torch of Reason (Silverton, Oregon)
   Truth Seeker (New York)
5) Many short tributes to Ingersoll which were published
   upon his death. These were published in magazines
   of many types.
6) Law briefs by Ingersoll, many of which were published
   by law printers. Some of the more important jury
   speeches are found in volume 10 of the Dresden Edition.
7) Books containing a few short (under two pages) quotes
   or excerpts from Ingersoll's writings.

How to Use This Checklist

The Checklist is divided into six major categories, which are:

I. *Separately Published Works by Ingersoll*

These include all separately published lectures, speeches, and essays. The entries are alphabetically arranged by the title used in the Dresden Edition. Where no equivalent DE title was found, the title of the separate publication is used. The editions of a work published by different publishers are listed under the standard title in order of the date of publication; those with the same contents but variant titles are listed last, again chronologically by publication date *within each title*. The Index lists both the standard and variant titles. A sample entry follows:

17 THE DEVIL (DE 4:353-419)

    a) C. P. Farrell, New York, 1899, 66p. ["The Agnostic Library v. I #1."]
       DLC, NN, NcD.
    b) R. Forder, London, 1899, 47p.
       NN.
    c) Freethought Publishing Co., London, [1899].
    d) Truth Seeker Co., New York, [c1899].
    e) Peter Eckler, New York, [c1899]. ON THE DEVIL.

The Dresden Edition listing gives the reader the location of this work within that collection: volume 4, pages 353-419. Items which could not be located in the DE, but which may be there under a different title are indicated by "(Not in DE?)." Where there was no DE title (which occurs usually only with early pirated versions of lectures which RGI later combined with other lectures or dropped), the title of the pirated work itself is used. These entries are marked "(Not in DE)." DE listings are not given elsewhere in the checklist unless the excerpt appears only in the item listed (such as a periodical article) and in the Dresden Edition.

The entries list the publisher first because this is the feature which most differentiates between the editions listed. Within the same year or approximate date, the publications are listed in alphabetical order by publisher. Any of the publication information enclosed by brackets does not appear on the title page.

The location symbols are given at the end of the entry. The symbols used are those of the *Union List of Serials*, with a few additions. A complete list is given separately. When only one or two location symbols are present, it does not necessarily mean that the work is not available at other libraries. The absence of any symbol can mean either that the compiler was unable to locate a copy in the sources checked, in which case the entry will be marked with an asterisk, or that it was located in a private collection. The brackets surrounding a location symbol indicate that the book had been listed as being at that source but that the compiler could not find it there. The variant title is given in all caps at the end of the publication information but before the location symbol(s). Any additional information or annotation is enclosed in brackets.

II. *Works with Contributions by Ingersoll*

Included here are both authorized and unauthorized
contributions which are complete articles or lectures; for
example, books for which Ingersoll wrote the preface,
collections containing a single RGI lecture, and even a few
critical works that contain an entire lecture. Compendia of
famous speeches and books on oratory which include an
Ingersoll speech as an example are *not* included in this
checklist for reasons mentioned in the Introduction. Works
containing short excerpts of RGI material are also not given.
The listings are arranged alphabetically by the title of the work.

III. *Ingersoll's Contributions to Periodicals*

This section is arranged by the year of the publication of the
articles. Annotations giving such relevant information as
the first appearance of a particular article in a certain
newspaper is given where it was obtainable. Items are noted
as initial publications only where it was verifiable. The city of
origin of a periodical is listed with its first chronological
appearance if it is small, obscure, easily confused with another,
or not listed in the ULS.

IV. *Collected Essays and Works by Ingersoll*

Included here are multi-volume collections as well as one
volume collections containing more than two essays by RGI.
The entries are given in alphabetical order by title. Even
though the identical title is used for several collections (such
as *Complete Works of Robert G. Ingersoll*), the contents
are not necessarily the same. The Dresden Edition is given as
the first entry because it is the only authorized version of
the complete works.

V. *Translations of Works by Ingersoll*

Entries are arranged by title. Where necessary the transliterated version of the title is used. A translation of the title appears in brackets at the end of the entry.

VI. *Works About Ingersoll*

    A. Biographical books and pamphlets arranged alphabetically by author.

    B. Periodical articles arranged alphabetically by author.

    C. Non-biographical books and pamphlets arranged alphabetically by author.

The Index gives a complete listing of all of the titles contained in the Checklist.

Since many editions and reprintings were made of most of Ingersoll's writings, especially those published by C. P. Farrell, only the date of the first edition or printing is given. Usually very few, if any, changes were apparently made between "editions." Significant ones are noted where possible.

Where newspaper references are given the dates may not be exact because the original references in the Dresden Edition were compiled from clippings in the Ingersoll family scrapbooks. Over one hundred of these scrapbooks filled with clippings may be found along with the Ingersoll papers in the Library of Congress. Often the dates were omitted or incorrectly noted for the clippings.

Great care must be taken with some of the English publications, especially those published by the "Freethought Publishing Company" of London. Those with this imprint published before 1890 were by Annie Besant and Charles Bradlaugh's "Freethought Publishing Company." Those published after 1890 with the same imprint (sometimes with the addition of "Ltd." after the name) were by G. W. Foote. These two companies are not identical or even related.

Ingersoll Chronology:

Date of First Delivery of Lectures & of First
Publication of Discussions

1860
& '64 PROGRESS (not published until after 1899)
1869 HUMBOLDT
1870 THOMAS PAINE (lecture)
1872 THE GODS
1874 INDIVIDUALITY
1874 HERETICS AND HERESIES
1877 THE GHOSTS
1877 LIBERTY OF MAN, WOMAN AND CHILD
1877 VINDICATION OF THOMAS PAINE (discussion)
1877 MY REVIEWERS REVIEWED (one-time-only lecture)
1877 ABOUT FARMING IN ILLINOIS
1878 ROBERT BURNS
1878 HARD TIMES AND THE WAY OUT
1879 MY CHICAGO BIBLE CLASS (newspaper discussion)
1879 SOME MISTAKES OF MOSES
1880 WHAT MUST WE DO TO BE SAVED?
1881 SOME REASONS WHY
1881 THE GREAT INFIDELS
1881 THE CHRISTIAN RELIGION (Ingersoll-Black)

Abbreviations

A	Appendix
c	Circa
DE	Dresden Edition
L	Leaves
LMWC	"Liberty of Man, Woman and Child"
[location]	Work not located at that library when checked.
NAR	*North American Review*
n. d.	No date of publication indicated
n. p.	No publisher indicated
n. place	No place of publication indicated
n. s.	New series
p	Page(s)
RGI	Robert G. Ingersoll
tr.	Translator
WMWDTBS	"What Must We Do to Be Saved?"
?	Identification, location, date, publisher, or place uncertain
[ ]	Information enclosed not actually present on title page
*	Publication not actually seen.

Location Symbols

CLSU	University of Southern California, Los Angeles
CSmH	Huntington Library, San Marino, California
CSt	Stanford University, Palo Alto, California
CU	University of California at Berkeley
CoU	University of Colorado, Boulder
CtY	Yale University, New Haven, Connecticut
DA	National Library of Agriculture, Washington, D. C.
DL	Divson Library, Sydney, Australia
DLC	Library of Congress, Washington, D. C.
EBM	British Museum, London
FC	Ferguson Collection, Sydney, Australia
FMU	University of Miami, Coral Gables, Florida
FTaSU	Florida State University, Tallahassee
IaU	University of Iowa, Iowa City
IaAS	Iowa State University, Ames
ICJ	John Crerar Library, Chicago
ICN	Newberry Library, Chicago
ICRL	Midwest Interlibrary Center, Chicago
ICU	University of Chicago, Illinois
IEN	Northwestern University, Evanston, Illinois
IHi	Illinois Historical Society, Springfield
IMunS	St. Mary of the Lake Seminary, Mundelein, Illinois
IU	University of Illinois, Urbana

InU	Indiana University, Bloomington
KU	University of Kansas, Lawrence
KyLE	Library Extension Division, Frankfort, Kentucky
KyWAT	Asbury Theological Seminary, Wilmore, Kentucky
LU	Louisiana State University, Baton Rouge
M	Massachusetts State Library, Boston
MB	Boston Public Library, Massachusetts
MH	Harvard University, Cambridge, Massachusetts
ML	Mitchell Library, Sydney, Australia
MWA	American Antiquarian Society, Worcester, Massachusetts
MdBE	Enoch Pratt Library, Baltimore, Maryland
MiD	Detroit Public Library, Michigan
MiU	University of Michigan, Ann Arbor
MnU	University of Minnesota, Minneapolis
MoKU	University of Kansas City, Missouri
MoU	University of Missouri, Columbia
MsU	University of Mississippi, Oxford
N	New York State Library, Albany
NBuG	Grosvenor Public Library, Buffalo, New York
NBuU	University of Buffalo, New York
NIC	Cornell University, Ithaca, New York
NL	National Library of Australia, Canberra
NN	New York City Public Library
NNC	Columbia University, New York City
NNUT	Union Theological Seminary, New York City
NNUW	New York University, Washington Square, New York City
NRU	University of Rochester, New York
NcD	Duke University, Durham, North Carolina
NcU	University of North Carolina, Chapel Hill
NjP	Princeton University, New Jersey
NjR	Rutgers University, New Brunswick, New Jersey

O	Ohio State Library, Columbus
OBlC	Bluffton College, Bluffton, Ohio
OC	Cincinnati Public Library, Ohio
OCH	Hebrew Union College, Cincinnati, Ohio
OCHi	Cincinnati Historical Society, Ohio
OCU	University of Cincinnati, Ohio
OCl	Cleveland Public Library, Ohio
OClW	Western Reserve University, Cleveland, Ohio
OClWHi	Western Reserve (i.e., Cleveland) Historical Society, Ohio
OCo	Columbus Public Library, Ohio
OD	Dayton Public Library, Ohio
OFH	Hayes Memorial Library, Fremont, Ohio
OHi	Ohio Historical Society, Columbus
OO	Oberlin College, Ohio
OT	Toledo Public Library, Ohio
OU	Ohio State University, Columbus
OkU	University of Oklahoma, Norman
OrCS	Oregon State University, Corvallis
OrU	University of Oregon, Eugene
PCC	Crozer Theological Seminary, Chester, Pennsylvania
PHC	Haverford College, Pennsylvania
PLF	Franklin & Marshall College, Lancaster, Pennsylvania
PP	Philadelphia Public Library, Pennsylvania
PPAmP	American Philosophical Society, Philadelphia, Pennsylvania
PPTU	Temple University, Philadelphia, Pennsylvania
PPWa	Wagner's Free Institute, Philadelphia, Pennsylvania
PPiU	University of Pittsburgh, Pennsylvania
PSt	Pennsylvania State University, University Park
PU	University of Pennsylvania, Philadelphia
RPB	Brown University, Providence, Rhode Island

TNJ	Joint University Libraries, Nashville, Tennessee
TU	University of Tennessee, Knoxville
TxDaM	Southern Methodist University, Dallas, Texas
TxLT	Texas Technological College, Lubbock
TxU	University of Texas, Austin
V	Virginia State Library, Richmond
ViU	University of Virginia, Charlottesville
WaU	University of Washington, Seattle

I. Separately Published Titles by Ingersoll

1 ABOUT THE HOLY BIBLE (DE 3:453-519)

  a) C. P. Farrell, New York, 1894, 73p.
    ["The Agnostic Library"]
    DLC, MiU, NIC, NcD, OO, PPTU.
  b) R. Forder, London, 1894, 59p.
    NN.
 *c) Banner of Light, Boston, [c1899].
 *d) Peter Eckler, New York, [c1889].
 *e) Truth Seeker Co., New York, [c1899].
 *f) Freethought Publishing Co., London, [189?]. THE
    HOLY BIBLE.
  g) Haldeman-Julius, Girard, Kansas, [1948?], 24p. THE
    TRUTH ABOUT THE HOLY BIBLE.
    KU, NN.
  h) n.p., New York, [19—], 32p. THE BIBLE
    NN.

2 A FEW REASONS FOR DOUBTING THE
  INSPIRATION OF THE BIBLE (DE 11:581-607)

  a) Truth Seeker Co., New York, 1899, 37p.
    NcD, NN.
 *b) C. P. Farrell, New York, [c1903].
  c) Pioneer Press, London, [1923], 16p. WHAT IS IT

1

WORTH? [Later title is THE BIBLE: WHAT IS IT
WORTH?]
NN.

d) Haldeman-Julius, Girard, Kansas, 1925, 32p. REASONS
FOR DOUBTING THE INSPIRATION OF THE
BIBLE. ["Little Blue Book #236." Also called SIXTY-ONE
REASONS FOR DOUBTING THE BIBLE.]

3 ABRAHAM LINCOLN (DE 3:123-173)

a) R. Forder, London, 1893, 30p.
CSmH, CtY, DLC, ICU, MH, OClWHi, RPB.

b)C. P. Farrell, New York, 1894, 53p.
CSmH, DLC, ICN, KU, MB, MiU, NN, ND, OClWHi,
OCo, OrU, RPB.

c) J. Lane Co., New York, 1894, 100p. [Authorized by
permission of C. P. Farrell.]
CU, DLC, ICRL, MH, MiD, OC, OCl, OClWHi, OCU,
OT, OkU, OT, PP, PP, RPB, ViU.

*d) Banner of Light, Boston, [c1899].

*e) Peter Eckler, New York, [c1899].

f) Exit Enterprises, [New York], 1968, 54L. [Offset of DE.]

g) G. S. Baldwin, Chicago, [1882], 13p. INGERSOLL ON
ABRAHAM LINCOLN.
DLC, NIC.

h) n.p., New York, 1896. THE RELIGIOUS BELIEF OF
ABRAHAM LINCOLN.
ICU.

i) Appeal Publishing Co., Girard, Kansas, [c1920], 57p.
LECTURE ON LINCOLN ["Appeal Pocket Series
#213."]
DLC, OClWHi, OFH, RPB.

4 ADDRESS BEFORE THE NEW YORK UNITARIAN
  CLUB [The Ideal] (DE 12:147-161)

 *a) Truth Seeker Co., New York, [c1899].
    [MB]
 *b) C. P. Farrell, New York, [c1903].
  c) n.p., Buffalo, N. Y., n.d., 12p.
    MB.
  d) Progressive Publishing Co., London, 1892, 16p. TRUE
    RELIGION.
 *e) Freethought Publishing Co., London, [189-]. TRUE
    RELIGION.

5 BIBLE IDOLATRY (Not in DE?)

  a) Truth Seeker Co., New York, [c1890], 8p.
    DLC, NN.
  b) C. P. Farrell, New York, [c1903].
    NN.

6 BLASPHEMY [Delivered in Brooklyn, Feb. 22, 1885]
  (Not in DE)

  a) Progressive Publishing Co., London, 1885, 16p.
    REAL BLASPHEMY.
    EBM.
 *b) Freethought Publishing Co., London, [189?].
    REAL BLASPHEMY.

7 TO THE BROOKLYN DIVINES (DE 7:169-215)

  a) Progressive Publishing Co., London, [c1885], 16p.
    THE CLERGY AND COMMON SENSE.
    DLC, NN.
  b) Freethought Publishing Co., London, [c1895]. THE
    CLERGY AND COMMON SENSE.

    c) Truth Seeker Co., New York, 1897, 122p. TO THE
CLERGY. ["Truth Seeker Library #59." Also contains
"Thomas Paine" and "God in the Constitution."]
NN.

  *d) C. P. Farrell, New York, [c1903]. TO THE CLERGY.

    e) Truth Seeker Co., New York, [1897], 122p.
INGERSOLL TO THE CLERGY.
NN.

  *f) Peter Eckler, New York, [c1899]. INGERSOLL TO
THE CLERGY.

  *g) C. P. Farrell, New York, [1898?]. HOW THE CHURCH
MEETS THE DEMANDS OF THE HOUR.

8 CHILDREN OF THE STAGE (DE 12:201-204)

    a) New York Anti-vivisection Society, New York, [1910?],
6p. [Pages numbered 201-204, 473-474. Also contains
A LETTER ON VIVISECTION (DE 11:473-474).
"Souvenir, Actors' Fund Fair, 1910."]

9 THE CHRISTIAN RELIGION [Ingersoll-Black Discussion]
(DE 6:3-117)

    a) Abel Heywood & Son, [Manchester, England], 1881,
107p. ["Leek Bijou Freethought Reprints."]
EBM, MoKU, NN.

    b) North American Review Co., New York, 1882, 143p.
CtY, ICRL, MiU, NNUW, OO, PCC.

    c) Freethought Publishing Co., London, 1883, 16p.
[Pages numbered 33-48.]
EBM.

    d) C. P. Farrell, New York, 1886, 117p.
IU, OCl.

    e) R. Forder, London, 1893, 23p.
NN, TxU.

*f) Banner of Light, Boston, [c1899].
*g) Peter Eckler, New York, [c1899].
 h) Morton & Co., Toronto, 1881, 22p. INGERSOLL
    DEMOLISHED BY JUDGE BLACK.
    MB.
 i) Freethought Publishing Co., London, 1883, 16p.
    IS ALL OF THE BIBLE INSPIRED? [Also in 2 parts
    of 16p. each. Robert G. Ingersoll's 2nd reply to
    Judge Black only.]
    ICN, NcD.

10 CIVIL RIGHTS SPEECH (DE 11:1-52)

 a) C. P. Farrell, New York, 1883, 53p.
 b) Truth Seeker Co., New York, [1899].

11 THE CREED OF SCIENCE (DE 4:290)

 *a) C. P. Farrell, New York, [c1899], 1 sheet [cardboard
     wall hanging].

12 CREEDS AND SPIRITUALITY [From *The Twentieth
   Century* via the New York *Morning Advertiser*.
   "Spirituality" is from *Conservator*, 1891] (DE 8:461-469;
   11:481-485)

 a) Progressive Publishing Co., London, 1891, 15p.
    NN.

13 CRIMES AGAINST CRIMINALS (DE 11:143-166)

 a) C. P. Farrell, New York, 1890, 40p.
    CSmH, IHi, MH, NIC, NN, NcD, OCl, OCo, OHi.
 b) Progressive Publishing Co., London, 1890, 29p.
    NN.
 *c) A. T. Wilson, Melbourne [Australia], 1890, 16p.
     NL.

*d) Truth Seeker Co., New York, [c1890].
*e) Freethought Publishing Co., London, [c1895].
*f) Banner of Light, Boston, [c1899].
*g) Peter Eckler, New York, [c1899].
　h) Roycrofters, East Aurora, N. Y., 1906, 59p.
　　 CSt, CtY, DLC, EBM, ICN, ICU, IEN, MB, MH, MdBE,
　　 NN, ViU.
　i) Haldeman-Julius, Girard, Kansas, [1925], 32p.
　　 ["Little Blue Book #139."]
*j) J. S. Ogilvie, New York, 1928.
　k) Phoenix Publishing Co., Baltimore, [19—], 32p.
　　 NjP.

14 DECLARATION OF THE FREE (DE 4:415-419)

　a) n.p., San Francisco, 1899, 2L. [On cardboard.
　　 "Souvenir Edition."]
　　 CSmH.
　b) C. P. Farrell, New York, [c1903], 1p. [An 18 couplet
　　 poem on card stock.]
　　 DLC.

15 DECLARATION OF INDEPENDENCE [Centennial
　 Oration] and A VISION OF WAR (DE 9:63-93, 167-170)

　a) C. P. Farrell, New York, 1895, 30p.
　b) Truth Seeker Co., New York, [c1899], 30p.
　c) Transcript Steambook & Job Co., Peoria, Illinois, 1876,
　　 15p. THE MEANING OF THE DECLARATION,
　　 A CENTENNIAL ORATION. [Also contains a
　　 speech nominating James G. Blaine.]
　　 OCHi.
　d) [Baldwin's Bookstore], Chicago, [1876?], 7p.
　　 DECLARATION OF INDEPENDENCE [only].
*e) n.p. New York, 1877. DECLARATION OF

INDEPENDENCE.
[MH].
*f) Truth Seeker Co., New York, 1894. CENTENNIAL
ORATION.
g) C. P. Farrell, New York, 1899, 15 L. [Illustrated
by H. A. Ogden.] A VISION OF WAR [only].
DLC, NN.

16 DECORATION DAY ADDRESS (DE 9:419-434)

*a) n.p., [New York, 1882]. COL. INGERSOLL'S
MEMORIAL ORATION.
[NN].
*b) Freethought Publishing Co., London, [188?].
DECORATION DAY.
[NN].

17 THE DEVIL (DE 4:353-419)

a) C. P. Farrell, New York, 1899, 66p. ["The Agnostic
Library vol. I #1."]
DLC, NN, NcD.
b) R. Forder, London, 1899, 47p.
NN.
*c) Freethought Publishing Co., London, [1899].
*d) Truth Seeker Co., New York, [c1899].
*e) Peter Eckler, New York, [c1899]. ON THE DEVIL.

18 DIFFICULTIES OF BELIEF [An Early Lecture]
(Not in DE?)

a) R. Forder, London, 1892, 16p.
ICN.
b) Freethought Publishing Co., London, 1892, 18p.
ICN.
c) W. H. Morrish, Bristol [England], n.d., 18p.

19 ERNEST RENAN [From *NAR*, 1892] (DE 11:283-301)

   a) R. Forder, London, 1892, 15p. ERNEST RENAN
AND JESUS CHRIST.
ICN, NN.

   b) Freethought Publishing Co., London, [c1895].
ERNEST RENAN AND JESUS CHRIST.

20 FAITH THAT SURELY WANES [Gov. Rollins' Fast Day
Proclamation] (DE 11:547-559)

   a) [Truth Seeker Co., New York, c1899], 15p. ["Truth
Seeker Tract ns #35."]
NN.

  *b) C. P. Farrell, New York, [c1903].

21 ABOUT FARMING IN ILLINOIS (DE 1:401-438)

  *a) Freethought Publishing Co., London, [c1880]. FARM
LIFE IN AMERICA.

   b) W. H. Morrish, Bristol [England], n.d., 14p. FARM
LIFE IN AMERICA.
MoKU, NN.

22 THE FIELD-INGERSOLL DISCUSSION [Faith or
Agnosticism] [From *NAR*, 1887] (DE 6:121-218)

   a) The North American Review Co., New York,
[1888], 83p.
DLC.

  *b) Peter Eckler, New York, [c1899].

   c) Progressive Publishing Co., London, 1880, 16p.
GOD AND MAN. [Ingersoll's 2nd reply only.]
EBM, MoKU.

  *d) Freethought Publishing Co., London, [c1895]. GOD
AND MAN.

   e) Progressive Publishing Co., London, 1887, 32p. FAITH

AND FACT. [Ingersoll's reply only.]
EBM, MoKU, NN.

f) Freethought Publishing Co., London, [c1895], 30p.
FAITH AND FACT.

g) C. P. Farrell, New York, 1888, 96p. INGERSOLL-FIELD
DISCUSSION.

*h) Banner of Light, Boston, [c1899]. INGERSOLL-FIELD
CONTROVERSY.

i) Haldeman-Julius, Girard, Kansas, [1948?], 48p.
FAITH OR AGNOSTICISM?

j) Scott & Jopling, Toronto, 1887, 32p. ["3rd edition."]
AN OPEN LETTER TO COL. R. G. INGERSOLL
... WITH COL. R. G. INGERSOLL'S REPLY.

23 FLIGHT OF THE SHADOWS (Not in DE?)

a) W. H. Morrish, Bristol [England], [188?], 18p.
NN, TxU.

24 THE FOUNDATIONS OF FAITH (DE 4:239-292)

a) C. P. Farrell, New York, 1896, 56p. ["The
Agnostic Library."]
DLC, NBuG, NN, NcD.

b) R. Forder, London, 1896, 31p.

*c) Banner of Light, Boston, [c1899].

*d) Peter Eckler, New York, [c1899].

e) Haldeman-Julius, Girard, Kansas, [192-], 23p.
KU.

25 FREE SPEECH AND AN HONEST BALLOT [Speech
at Cooper Union, 1880] (Not in DE)

a) n.p., Chicago, 1880, 13p.

26 THE GHOSTS (DE 1:257-326)

   a) C. P. Farrell, Washington, D. C., 1878, 70p.
     DLC.
   b) Albany News Co., Albany, N. Y., [1878], 15p.
     MH, NN.
   c) Weed, Parsons & Co., [Albany, N. Y., 1878], 15p.
     MH.
   d) [G. S. Baldwin], Chicago, [c1880], 16p.
     IHi
   e) Freethought Publishing Co., London, 1881, 32p.
     [Also issued as 2 separate parts.]
     EBM.
   f) R. Forder, London, 1893, 31p.
   g) C. P. Farrell, New York, 1910, 67p. [Pages numbered
     259-326.]
     NN, PP.
   h) Watts & Co., London, 1912, 32p.
     ICN.
  *i) J. S. Ogilvie, New York, 1928.
   j) Abel Heywood, Manchester [England], n.d., 24p.
   k) Haldeman-Julius, Girard, Kansas, n.d., 36p. THE
     TRUTH and GHOSTS.

27 GOD IN THE CONSTITUTION (DE 11:121-134)

   a) Truth Seeker Co., New York, [c1899], 17p.
  *b) C. P. Farrell, New York, [c1903].
  *c) Freethought Publishing Co., London, [c1895].
     GOD AND THE STATE.
   d) Progressive Publishing Co., London, 1896, 31p. GOD
     AND THE STATE.

28 THE GODS (DE 1:7-90)

   a) J. Braithwaite, Dundein [Scotland], 1880, 23p.
     CtY.

b) C. P. Farrell, New York, [c1903], 90p.
NBuG, NN, NjP.
c) Haldeman-Julius, Girard, Kansas, [1925], 64p. ["Little
Blue Book #185."]
d) Transcript Book & Job Print, Peoria, Illinois, 1872,
73p. [First Edition.] AN ORATION ON THE GODS.
DLC, InU, NN, OCHi, ViU.
e) Daily Bulletin Steam Book & Job Print, Cairo, Illinois,
1873. AN ORATION ON THE GODS.
OCHi.
f) D. M. Bennett, New York, 1876, 60p. ORATION ON
THE GODS. ["Truth Seeker Tract #2."]
DLC.
g) Freethought Publishing Co., London, 1877, 42p.
ORATION ON THE GODS. [1887 version entitled
HOW MAN MAKES GODS, 16p.]
EBM.
h) A. Besant & C. Bradlaugh, London, 1883, 40p.
ORATION ON THE GODS.
ICN.
i) n.p., New York, [188?], 8p. ["Published For the
Trade."] ORATION ON THE GODS.
NN.
j) R. Forder, London, 1893, 47p. ORATION ON THE
GODS.
NN.
k) John Heywood, Manchester [England], n.d., 16p.
THE GODS: PAST AND PRESENT.

29 GOLD SPEECH [The Chicago and New York Gold
Speech] (DE 9:535-582)

a) C. P. Farrell, New York, [c1903], 89p. [Pages
numbered 307-395.]

b) John F. Higgins, Chicago, 1896, 29p. INSPIRES
TO LOYALTY.

c) n.p., n. place, n.d., 24p. SOUND SENSE ON SOUND
MONEY.
CU.

30 GREAT INFIDELS (DE 3:307-395)

a) n.p., Chicago, [1881?], 8p. ["Published for the Trade."]
ICL.

*b) C. P. Farrell, New York, [c1899]. [Later eds. pages
numbered 309-395.]
NcD.

c) John Heywood, Manchester [England], n.d., 12p.
[Pages numbered 51-62.]
MoKU.

d) Freethought Publishing Co., London, 1887, 16p.
SAVIORS OF THE WORLD. [Also contains 2 short
speeches. Pages numbered 145-160.]

e) Haldeman-Julius, Girard, Kansas, n.d., 30p. WHAT
GREAT INFIDELS HAVE DONE TO ADVANCE
CIVILIZATION.
NN.

31 THE GREAT INGERSOLL CONTROVERSY [About
the Christmas Sermon by RGI] (DE 7:263-355)

a) Brandus & Co., New York, 1892, 213p.
EBM.

b) J. Buckley, New York, [1892], 256p.
EBM, OO.

c) Peter Eckler, New York, 1894, 123p.
KU.

*d) C. P. Farrell, New York, [c1899].

e) Haldeman-Julius, Girard, Kansas, 1949, 30p. A

CHRISTMAS SERMON (AND THE CONTROVERSY
IT AROUSED).

32 HARD TIMES AND THE WAY OUT (DE 9:267-302)

  a) Gibson Brothers, Washington, D. C., 1878, 24p.
    DLC, ICJ, MH, OO.
  b) West End Printing House, Washington, D. C., 1878, 24p.
    NN, OCHi.
 *c) C. P. Farrell, New York, [c1903].

33 HELL (Not in DE?)

  a) E. McCormack, New York, [1878?], 16p.
    MB, NN.
 *b) n.p., [Cincinnati?], [c1880], 13p.
    EBM.
  c) Freethought Publishing Co., London, 1883, 32p.
    EBM.
  d) R. Forder, London, 1891, 32p. [Pages numbered 17-49.]
  e) n.p., n. place, n.d., 15p. HELL and INGERSOLL'S
    SHORTER CATECHISM. ["Published for the Trade."]
    CSmH.
  f) Wheeler, King & Co., Edinburgh, n.d., 16p. HELL—
    WARM WORDS ON THE CHEERFUL AND
    COMFORTING DOCTRINE OF ETERNAL
    DAMNATION.
  g) Abel Heywood & Son, Manchester [England], n.d., 20p.
    HELL—WARM WORDS ON THE CHEERFUL
    AND COMFORTING DOCTRINE OF ETERNAL
    DAMNATION.
  h) Freethought Publishing Co., London, 1884, 14p.
    DIVINE VIVISECTION or HELL.
  i) A. & H. Bradlaugh Bonner, London, 1892, 16p. [Pages
    numbered 17-32.] DIVINE VIVISECTION or HELL.

j) W. H. Morrish, Bristol [England], [c1885], 18p.
HEREAFTER. [Includes "Great Infidels."]
TxU.

34 HERETICS AND HERESIES (DE 1:210-253)

a) Baldwin's Bookstore, Chicago, [1874?], 14p.
ICU, N.
b) D. M. Bennett, New York, 1876, 32p. ["Truth
Seeker Tract #3."]
DLC.
c) Freethought Publishing Co., London, [1877], 24p.
EBM.
d) C. P. Farrell, New York, 1910, 45p. [Pages numbered
209-253.]

35 THE HOUSEHOLD OF FAITH [i.e., "The Divided
Household of Faith"] (DE 11:215-233)

a) Progressive Publishing Co., London, 1888, 16p.
EBM, ICN, NN.
*b) Freethought Publishing Co., London, [c1895].
c) Pioneer Press, London, [1922], 16p.
NN.

36 HOW TO REFORM MANKIND (DE 4:115-156)

a) C. P. Farrell, New York, 1896, 55p.
CSmH, DLC, NN, NcD.
*b) Peter Eckler, New York, [c1899].
*c) Banner of Light, Boston, [c1899].
d) Watts & Co., London, 1913, 24p.
ICN.
e) R. Forder, London, 1896, 29p. THE COMING
CIVILISATION.
ICN, NN.

37 HUMBOLDT (DE 1:93-117)

a) D. M. Bennett, New York, 1876, 17p. HUMBOLDT and HERETICS AND HERESIES. ["Truth Seeker Tract #6."]
DLC.

b) Peter Eckler, New York, 1890, 72p. HUMBOLDT and HERETICS AND HERESIES.

c) C. P. Farrell, New York, 1910, 71p. [Pages numbered 93-117, 209-253.] HUMBOLDT and HERETICS AND HERESIES.
NN, NcD.

d) Transcript Co., Peoria, Illinois, 1869, 22p. AN ORATION DELIVERED AT PEORIA, ILLINOIS AT THE UNVEILING OF A STATUE OF HUMBOLDT. [First Robert G. Ingersoll in print.]
MB, MH.

e) [G. S. Baldwin], Chicago, [1869?], 7p. PHILOSOPHER OF REASON: HUMBOLDT. ["Published for the Trade."]
N.

f) Freethought Publishing Co., London, [1877], 14p. ORATION ON HUMBOLDT.
EBM.

g) Freethought Publishing Co., London, [1887], 16p. LAW, NOT GOD.

38 INAUGURAL ADDRESS (Not in DE?)

*a) C. P. Farrell, New York, [c1899].
*b) Truth Seeker Co., New York, [c1899].

39 TO THE INDIANAPOLIS CLERGY [From *The Iconoclast*, 1882] (DE 7: 125-167)

*a) C. P. Farrell, New York, [c1899].

b) Vincent Publishing Co., Indianapolis, 1893, 64p.
OPEN LETTER TO INDIANAPOLIS CLERGYMEN.
[Also contains "The Genesis of Life" by W. H. Lamaster.]
NN.

40 INDIVIDUALITY (DE 1:169-206)

a) C. P. Farrell, New York, 1897, 36p. [Pages numbered
170-206.]
NN.
b) D. M. Bennett, New York, 1876, 17p. ["Truth Seeker
Tract #4."] ARRAIGNMENT OF THE CHURCH.
DLC.
c) Freethought Publishing Co., London, [1877], 16p.
ARRAIGNMENT OF THE CHURCH AND A PLEA
FOR INDIVIDUALITY.
EBM.
d) Freethought Publishing Co., London, 1883, 16p. TAKE
A ROAD OF YOUR OWN or INDIVIDUALITY
AND MENTAL FREEDOM.
EBM.
e) R. Forder, London, 1892, 16p. TAKE A ROAD OF
YOUR OWN or INDIVIDUALITY AND MENTAL
FREEDOM.

41 INGERSOLL CATECHISED (DE 8:206-216)

a) C. P. Farrell, Washington, D. C., 1884, 11p. [Also
contains "The Birthplace of Burns," a poem by
Robert G. Ingersoll, on last page.]
EBM, NN.
*b) Freethought Publishing Co., London, [c1890]. THE
GREAT MISTAKE.
c) G. W. Foote, London, n.d., 8p. THE GREAT MISTAKE.
ICN.

42 INGERSOLL ON McGLYNN (DE 8:284-291)

a) Truth Seeker Co., New York, [c1887], 8p.
NN.
b) Washington *Post*, Washington, D. C., 1887, 8p.
DR. McGLYNN AND THE ROMAN CATHOLIC
CHURCH.
DLC.

43 INGERSOLL-GLADSTONE CONTROVERSY ON
CHRISTIANITY [Colonel Ingersoll on Christianity]
[From a series in *NAR*] (DE 6:221-303)

a) C. P. Farrell, New York, [1888?], 72p. [Pages
numbered 109-182.]
MH, NN.
*b) Peter Eckler, New York, [c1899].
*c) Banner of Light, Boston, [c1899].
d) Progressive Publishing Co., London, 1888, 47p. REPLY
TO GLADSTONE. [Contains biography of Robert G.
Ingersoll by J. M. Wheeler.]
EBM.
e) Freethought Publishing Co., London, 1899, 47p. REPLY
TO GLADSTONE. [Introduction by G. W. Foote.]
NN, OFH.
f) Haldeman-Julius, Girard, Kansas, [1920], 96p.
CONTROVERSY ON CHRISTIANITY. ["Little
Blue Book #130," also as "People's Pocket Series #130"]

44 LAY SERMON ON THE LABOR QUESTION
(DE 4:211-235)

*a) C. P. Farrell, New York, [c1886].
*b) Banner of Light, Boston, [c1899].
*c) Commonwealth Co., New York, [c1902].

d) Truth Seeker Co., New York, 1886, 25p. A LAY
   SERMON.
   DLC, InU, PPWa.

e) Progressive Publishing Co., London, [1888], 16p.
   SOCIAL SALVATION, A LAY SERMON.
   EBM, ICN.

f) Freethought Publishing Co., London, [c1895]. SOCIAL
   SALVATION.

45 LIBERTY IN LITERATURE [Testimonial to Walt
   Whitman] (DE 3:251-304)

a) Truth Seeker Co., New York, 1890, 77p. [The 1892 ed.
   also contains Robert G. Ingersoll's address at
   Walt Whitman's funeral.]
   CU, DLC, EBM, NIC, NN, NcD, NcU, OC, OCl, PP,
   PU, ViU.

b) Gay & Bird, London, 1891, 77p.
   CSt, EBM.

*c) C. P. Farrell, New York, [c1903].

d) Progressive Publishing Co., London, 1890, 34p.
   CtY, RPB.

*e) Freethought Publishing Co., London, [c1895].
   ORATION ON WALT WHITMAN.

f) C. G. Burgoyne's Printing Business, New York, 1890,
   32L. TESTIMONIAL TO WALT WHITMAN.
   DLC.

g) Progressive Publishing Co., London, 1890, 34p.
   WREATHE THE LIVING BROWS.
   CSmH, DLC, MB, NN, ViU, WaU.

46 LIBERTY OF MAN, WOMAN AND CHILD (DE
1:329-398)

a) Albany News Co., Albany, N. Y. [1877], 15p.
[Double column pages.]
MH, NN, OHi, OO.

*b) Freethought Publishing Co., London, [c1880].

c) C. P. Farrell, New York, 1895, 72p. [Pages numbered
70-142. Later edition's pages numbered 329-398.]
DLC, MB, MiD, NcD, OO, OU, RPB.

*d) Banner of Light, Boston, [c1899].

*e) Peter Eckler, New York, [c1899].

f) Watts & Co., London, 1912, 44p.
ICN, NN.

*g) J. S. Ogilvie, New York, 1928.

h) Haldeman-Julius, Girard, Kansas, [1948?], 23p.

i) D. M. Bennett, New York, [c1875], 21p. LIBERTY FOR
MAN, WOMAN AND CHILD.

j) Spencer Ellis, Toronto, 1891, 16p. LIBERTY FOR
MAN, WOMAN AND CHILD.
OClWHi.

*k) H. J. Franklin, Sydney, [Australia], 1881, 16p.
WOMAN, PRIEST AND DEVIL.
FC.

l) Freethought Publishing Co., London, 1884, Parts I & II,
16p. each. HUMAN LIBERTY; or INTELLECTUAL
DEVELOPMENT.
EBM, ICN.

*m) Freethought Publishing Co., London, [188?]. THE
RELIGION OF THE FUTURE.

n) W. H. Morrish, Bristol [England], [189?], 18p. THE
RELIGION OF THE FUTURE.
NN, TxU.

    o) n.p., Seattle, Washington, [1916], 7p. LIBERTY OF
THE CHILD.
NN.

    p) [Baldwin's, Chicago], n.d. ["Published for the Trade."]
COL. INGERSOLL'S LECTURE ON THE LMWC
and HIS ADDRESS AT THE FUNERAL OF HIS
BROTHER.
OClWHi.

47 LIFE (DE 12:511-512)

    *a) C. P. Farrell, New York, [c1903], 1L. [Cardboard
wall hanging.]

48 THE LIMITATIONS OF TOLERATION (DE 7:217-260)

    *a) C. P. Farrell, New York, 1889.
    b) Truth Seeker Co., New York, 1889, 44p.
ICRL, MH, NN.
    *c) Freethought Publishing Co., London, [c1895].
    d) Progressive Publishing Co., London, 1889, 30p.
THE LIMITS OF TOLERATION.
ICN, NN, NcD.

49 LIVE TOPICS [Interview from *Truth Seeker*, 1885]
(DE 8:248-263)

    a) Progressive Publishing Co., London, 1886, 16p.
EBM.
    b) R. Forder, London, 1886, 15p.
NN.
    *c) Freethought Publishing Co., London, [c1895].

50 A LOOK BACKWARD AND A PROPHECY [From
Truth Seeker, 1898] (DE 11:563-576)

    a) Truth Seeker Co., New York, [1898], 16p.
["Truth Seeker Tract ns #25."]
NN.

*b) C. P. Farrell, New York, [c1901].

51 LOVE (DE 2:420)

a) C. P. Farrell, New York, [c1903], 1L. folio. [A cardboard wall hanging containing photo of Robert G. Ingersoll & grandchildren.]

52 MODERN THINKERS [Preface by RGI to V. B. Denslow's book.] (DE 12:7-23)

a) Abel Heywood, Manchester [England], [18—], 19p. NcD.

b) Freethought Publishing Co., London, 1884, 16p. [Pages numbered 225-240.] THE SPIRIT OF THE AGE.

53 MYTH AND MIRACLE (DE 2:431-492)

a) Progressive Publishing Co., London, 1886, 15p. EBM, ICN, NcD.

b) R. Forder, London, 1893, 15p.

c) C. P. Farrell, New York, 1895, 63p. DLC, MB, NcD.

d) Freethought Publishing Co., London, [c1895].

*e) Banner of Light, Boston, [c1899].

*f) Peter Eckler, New York, [c1899].

54 THE OATH QUESTION [From *Secular Review* (London), 1884] (DE 8:179-188)

a) Truth Seeker Co., New York, [189-], 11p. ["Truth Seeker Tracts ns #41."] NN.

*b) C. P. Farrell, New York, [c1903].

c) H. Cattell & Co., London, 1884. COL. INGERSOLL ON THE OATH QUESTION. DLC.

55 THE OLD AND THE NEW (Not in DE)

*a) Truth Seeker Co., New York, 1878. ["Truth Seeker Tract #100."]

56 OPENING SPEECH TO THE JURY [In the suit of B&M Telegraph vs Western Union] (Not in DE)

a) n.p., New York, 1886, 40p.
CtY, DLC, ICJ, ICN, IU, MB, MH, N, NN, NNC, PPAmP.
*b) Truth Seeker Co., New York, [c1890].
*c) C. P. Farrell, New York, [c1903].

57 ORTHODOXY (DE 2:341-427)

a) C. P. Farrell, Washington, D. C., 1884, 54p. [Later editions are 86p. with pages numbered 341-427.]
DCL, EBM, ICRL, NN, NcD.
*b) Truth Seeker Co., New York, 1884.
*c) Banner of Light, Boston, [c1899].
d) Baldwin's, Chicago, [1884], 16p. NEW LECTURE ON ORTHODOXY.
OClWHi.
e) Progressive Publishing Co., London, [1884], 32p. THE DYING CREED.
MoKU
f) G. W. Foote, London, [189-?], 32p. THE DYING CREED.
NN.
*g) Freethought Publishing Co., London, [189-?]. THE DYING CREED.
h) Haldeman-Julius, Girard, Kansas, [192-], 31p. DEATH BLOWS AT ORTHODOXY.
KU.

58 PERSONAL DEISM DENIED [An Early Lecture] (Not in DE)

   a) Abel Heywood & Son, Manchester [England], [188—], 16p. NcD.

59 PROFESSOR HUXLEY AND AGNOSTICISM [From *NAR*, 1889] (DE 11:263-279)

   a) Freethought Publishing Co., London, 1891, 13p. CHRIST AND MIRACLES. [Second half of *NAR* article only.] NcD.

   b) *Exit Magazine*, New York, 1968, 18L. HUXLEY AND AGNOSTICISM. [Offset of DE.]

60 PROGRESS (DE 4:423-476)

   *a) C. P. Farrell, New York, 1899. PROGRESS and WHAT IS RELIGION?

61 REPAIRING THE IDOLS [Interview on "Robert Elsmere," from New York *World*, Nov. 18, 1888] (DE 8:412-422)

   a) Progressive Publishing Co., London, 1888, 14p. EBM, NcD.

   *b) Freethought Publishing Co., London, [c1895].

62 A REVIEW OF THE SUGAR QUESTION (Not in DE)

   a) T. McGill & Co., Washington, D. C., [188-], 36p. DA, DLC.

63 MY REVIEWERS REVIEWED (DE 7:5-107)

   *a) C. P. Farrell, New York, [c1899].

   b) Haldeman-Julius, Girard, Kansas, [1949], 32p.

*c) Truth Seeker Co., New York, 1879. INGERSOLL'S
REVIEW OF HIS REVIEWERS. ["Truth Seeker Tract
#121."]

64 ROBERT BURNS (DE 3:77-119)

*a) C. P. Farrell, New York, [c1899].

65 ROME OR REASON [Ingersoll-Manning Discussion
From *NAR*, 1888] (DE 6:307-396)

  a) Progressive Publishing Co., London, 1888, 46p.
    EBM.
  b) Freethought Publishing Co., London, [c1895], 48p.
    EBM.
  c) C. P. Farrell, New York, 1898, 127p. [Also contains
    "Is Divorce Wrong?" Later ed. pages numbered 307-429.]
    DLC.
*d) Banner of Light, Boston, [c1899].
*e) Peter Eckler, New York, [c1899].
  f) Haldeman-Julius, Girard, Kansas, 1920, 64p. ["Little
    Blue Book #129."]
    DLC.
  g) G. W. Foote & Co. (Pioneer Press), London, 1931, 59p.
    EBM.

66 SHAKESPEARE (DE 3:1-73)

  a) C. P. Farrell, New York, 1891, 73p.
    CoU, DLC, MB, MH, MiD, MiU, NcD, NcU, OCl, OT,
    OU, PHC, ViU, WaU.
*b) Freethought Publishing Co., London, [c1895].
*c) Peter Eckler, New York, [c1899].
  d) R. Forder, London, [189-], 50p.
    MH, NN, NRU.
  e) Haldeman-Julius, Girard, Kansas, n.d., 26p.

SHAKESPEARE — THE GREATEST GENIUS OF
THE WORLD. [Also as People's Pocket Series #160
with title "A Lecture on Shakespeare."]

67 SHOULD INFIDELS SEND THEIR CHILDREN TO
SUNDAY SCHOOL? (DE 11:531-534)

a) Truth Seeker Co., New York, 1890, 4p. ADVICE TO
PARENTS TO KEEP CHILDREN OUT OF CHURCH
AND SUNDAY SCHOOL. ["Truth Seeker Tract
ns #50."]
NN.

68 SKULLS [From the latter part of "LMWC," probably
an early version] (Not in DE)

a) [G. S. Baldwin, Chicago, 1880], 16p.
IHi.
b) R. Forder, London, 1893, 29p.
ICN.
*c) Freethought Publishing Co., London, [c1895].
*d) J. S. Ogilvie, New York, 1928.
e) Abel Heywood & Sons, Manchester [England], n.d., 19p.

69 SOME MISTAKES OF MOSES (DE 2:1-270)

a) C. P. Farrell, Washington, D. C., 1879, 278p. [First
ed. Last 8p. are "A Tribute to Ebon C. Ingersoll."
Printed by Franks & Sons, Peoria, Illinois. This long
version is a combined anthology of the various lectures
given by Robert G. Ingersoll on this subject.]
DLC, EBM, OCl, OT, OU.
b) [Abel Heywood & Son, Manchester, Eng.] 1881, 218p.
["Leek Bijou Freethought Reprints."]
EBM.

c) Progressive Publishing Co., London, 1885, 136p.
   NcD.
d) C. P. Farrell, New York, 1888, 270p. ["Ninth Edition."
   Without the 8 page "Tribute," but otherwise apparently
   only the title page changed from 1879 version.]
   CSmH, DLC, MB, MiU, NN, NcD, NjP, OCHi,
   OHi, ViU.
e) Peter Eckler, New York, [c1890], 270p. [Apparently
   C. P. Farrell plates.]
*f) Banner of Light, Boston, [c1899].
g) Freethought Publishing Co., London, [189-], 132p.
   ["Only Complete Edition Published in England."]
h) Freethought Press Assn., New York, [c1945], 270p.
   [Apparently DE plates.]
   MsU, NBuG.
i) Haldeman-Julius, Girard, Kansas, [c1945], 92p.
   ["Big Blue Book" series.]
   IEN.
j) Berg & McCann, Chicago, 1879, 20p. MISTAKES
   OF MOSES.
   DLC, OO.
k) Freethought Publishing Co., London, [c1880], 16p.
   [Pages numbered 129-144. An incomplete (early)
   version. An 1883 edition has 31p.] MISTAKES
   OF MOSES.
   EBM.
*l) W. C. Rigby, Adelaide, [Australia], [c1880], 16p.
   MISTAKES OF MOSES.
   ML.
m) [G. S. Baldwin, Chicago, c1880], 16p. MISTAKES
   OF MOSES. ["Published for the Trade."]
   IHi, N.

n) R. Forder, London, 1883, 16p. [Pages numbered 129-144.] MISTAKES OF MOSES.

o) J. Heywood, London, [188-], 30p. MISTAKES OF MOSES.
NN.

p) L. Lipkind, New York, [188-], 32p. MISTAKES OF MOSES.
NN.

q) Baldwin's Bookstore, Chicago, [18—], 14p. MISTAKES OF MOSES.
DLC.

r) Pioneer Press, London, 1912, 31p. MISTAKES OF MOSES.
EBM.

s) Abel Haywood & Son, Manchester, [Eng.], n.d., 20p.

*t) W. H. Terry, Melbourne, [Australia], 1881, 20p. MOSES' MISTAKES.
DL.

70 SOME INTERROGATION POINTS (DE 11:181-199)

a) Commonwealth Co., New York, 1895, 6p. MAN AND MACHINE, an eloquent arraignment of the present social system. [Is only the last half of "Some Interrogation Points."]
InU, [NNUT].

71 SOME REASONS WHY (DE 2:273-334)

a) C. P. Farrell, New York, 1895, 64p.
NN, OO.

b) Banner of Light, Boston, [c1899.]

c) Peter Eckler, New York, [c1899].

d) Haldeman-Julius, Girard, Kansas, n.d., 19p. SOME REASONS WHY I AM A FREETHINKER.

72 STAGE AND PULPIT (DE 8:296-306) [From *Truth Seeker*, 1888]

  a) Truth Seeker Co., New York, 1887, 12p.
  NN.
  *b) C. P. Farrell, New York, [c1903].

73 IS SUICIDE A SIN? (DE 7:375-408)

  a) Standard Publishing Co., New York, 1894, 95p.
  DLC, NN, OClW, PP.
  b) C. P. Farrell, New York, 1895, 95p.
  c) Holland Publishing Co., New York, 1895, 95p.
  [With replies and rejoinders.]
  DLC.
  *d) Freethought Publishing Co., London, [c1895].
  *e) Banner of Light, Boston, [c1899].
  f) Peter Eckler, New York, [c1899]. 95p.
  DLC.
  g) R. Forder, London, 1894, 14p. LAST WORDS ON SUICIDE.
  h) Freethought Publishing Co., London, [c1895]. LAST WORDS ON SUICIDE.
  *i) Pioneer Press, London, [c1920]. IS SUICIDE A SIN and LAST WORDS ON SUICIDE.
  j) Haldeman-Julius, Girard, Kansas, [1949], 59p. ARGUMENTS IN SUPPORT OF SUICIDE.
  [20 pages are title articles plus 7 short pieces.]
  KU.

74 SUPERSTITION (DE 4:295-349)

  a) R. Forder, London, 1894, 14p. [Later eds. have 48p.]
  NN.
  *b) Freethought Publishing Co., London, [c1895].
  c) C. G. Burgoyne, New York, 1898, 62p.

d) C. P. Farrell, New York, 1898, 62p.
   DLC, NIC, NN.
*e) Peter Eckler, New York, [c1899].
 f) Haldeman-Julius, Girard, Kansas, [1948?], 20p.
   THE CRIME OF SUPERSTITION.

75 INTERVIEWS ON TALMAGE [*Talmagian Catechism*,
   DE 5:363-443] (DE 5:7-359)

*a) Peter Eckler, New York, [c1899].
 b) C. P. Farrell, Washington, D. C., 1882, 443p. SIX
   INTERVIEWS WITH RGI ON SIX SERMONS BY
   DeW. TALMAGE, D.D.
   DLC, EBM, ICU, IaU, NN, NcD, OCl, OCo, OHi, ViU.
 c) C. P. Farrell, New York, 1888, 443p. SIX INTERVIEWS
   WITH RGI ON SIX SERMONS BY DeW.
   TALMAGE, D.D.
   NN, ViU.
 d) J. Heywood, Manchester, [England], [1882], 16p.
   INGERSOLL'S TILT WITH TALMAGE.
   EBM, MoKU, TxU.
*e) Freethought Publishing Co., London, [c1885].
   TILT WITH TALMAGE.
*f) Banner of Light, Boston, [c1899]. SIX INTERVIEWS
   ON TALMAGE.
 g) Pioneer Press, London, 1903, 48p. A CHRISTIAN
   CATECHISM. [The "Talmagian Catechism"
   part only.]
   EBM, NN.
 h) Haldeman-Julius, Girard, Kansas, n.d., 104p. WHAT
   CAN YOU BELIEVE IN THE BIBLE? [Also 2p. on
   G. J. Holyoake.]
   KU.

i) James Burns & R. Forder, London, 1891, 16p.
COL. INGERSOLL'S REPLY.

76 TALMAGIAN THEOLOGY (Not in DE)

a) Progressive Publishing Co., London, 1889, 29p. DO
I BLASPHEME? [Other versions have 16p.]
NN.
b) R. Forder, London, 1893, 29p. DO I BLASPHEME?
NN.
*c) Freethought Publishing Co., London, [189?].
DO I BLASPHEME?

77 A THANKSGIVING SERMON (DE 4:159-208)

a) C. P. Farrell, New York, 1897, 78p. [Also contains
tribute to Henry Ward Beecher.]
DLC, NcD.
*b) Peter Eckler, New York, [c1899].

78 THOMAS PAINE (DE 1:121-165)

a) C. P. Farrell, New York, [1899?], 45p. [Pages
numbered 121-165.]
CU, KU, NN.
b) Transcript Book and Job Print, Peoria, Illinois, 1871,
41p. ORATION ON THE LIFE AND SERVICES
OF THOMAS PAINE.
DLC, NcD.
c) D. M. Bennett, New York, 1876, 31p. ORATION ON
THOMAS PAINE. ["Truth Seeker Tract #3."]
d) Freethought Publishing Co., London, [1877], 24p.
ORATION ON THOMAS PAINE.
EBM.
e) Freethought Publishing Co., London, [1877], 16p.
THE APOTHEOSIS OF THOMAS PAINE.

f) Truth Seeker Co., New York, 1879. THOMAS PAINE GLORIFIED. ["Truth Seeker Tract #163."]

g) G. Standring, London, 1883, 32p. THOMAS PAINE GLORIFIED.
EBM, MoKU.

*h) Freethought Publishing Co., London, [188?]. THOMAS PAINE THE REPUBLICAN.

i) R. Forder, London, 1892, 24p. PAINE THE PIONEER.
CtY, NN.

*j) Freethought Publishing Co., London, [189?]. PAINE THE PIONEER.

k) Progressive Publishing Co., London, 1892, 14p. HUMANITY'S DEBT TO THOMAS PAINE.
NN.

*l) Freethought Publishing Co., London, [189?]. HUMANITY'S DEBT TO THOMAS PAINE.

m) [Truth Seeker Co., New York, c1899], 34p. WHY WE HONOR THOMAS PAINE.
NN.

n) n.p., Chicago, [18—], 10p. LIFE AND DEEDS OF THOMAS PAINE.
CtY, MH.

79 THE THREE PHILANTHROPISTS [From *NAR*, 1891] (DE 11:343-353)

a) Progressive Publishing Co., London, 1892, 15p.
*b) Freethought Publishing Co., London, [c1895].

80 TOLSTOI AND THE "KREUTZER SONATA" [From *NAR*, 1890] (DE 11:305-318)

a) Progressive Publishing Co., London, 1890, 15p. LOVE THE REDEEMER.
NN.

*b) Freethought Publishing Co., London, [c1895].
LOVE THE REDEEMER.

81 THE TRIAL OF C. B. REYNOLDS FOR BLASPHEMY
[Defense summation by RGI] (DE 11:55-117)

a) C. P. Farrell, New York, 1888, 84p.
CtY, DLC, ICJ, IU, MiU, NN, NcD, WaU.
b) Haldeman-Julius, Girard, Kansas, n.d., 31p.
c) G. S. Baldwin, Chicago, [c1887], 14p. THE GREAT
JERSEY HERESY CASE.
d) Progressive Publishing Co., London, 1888, 60p.
DEFENCE OF FREETHOUGHT.
EBM, ICN.
e) Freethought Publishing Co., London, [c1895], 60p.
DEFENCE OF FREETHOUGHT.
EBM, NN.
*f) Banner of Light, Boston, [c1899]. BLASPHEMY.
*g) Peter Eckler, New York, [c1899]. BLASPHEMY.
*h) Truth Seeker Co., New York, [c1899]. BLASPHEMY.

82 TRIBUTE TO HIS BROTHER [Ebon C. Ingersoll]
(DE 12:389-391)

*a) Truth Seeker Co., New York, [c1899].
*b) C. P. Farrell, New York, [c1903].

83 TRIBUTE TO RICHARD H. WHITING (DE
12:441-442)

a) [Privately printed, New York?], 1888, 4p.

84 A TRIBUTE TO ROSCOE CONKLING (DE 12:427-437)

*a) C. P. Farrell, New York, 1888.
b) n.p., [Albany, N. Y.?], [1888], 16p.
NN.

c) Ivers & Co., New York, 1888, 24p. COL. INGERSOLL'S
MEMORIAL ORATION ON ROSCOE CONKLING.
EBM, IU, MiD, MiU, NN, OClW, OClWHi.

d) J. B. Lyon, Albany, N. Y., 1888, 95p. MEMORIAL
ADDRESS ON ROSCOE CONKLING.
DLC.

e) Troy Press Co., Troy, N. Y., 1888, 38p. MATCHLESS
EULOGY ON ROSCOE CONKLING.
OCl.

f) G. S. Baldwin, Chicago, [c1888], 12p. MATCHLESS
EULOGY ON ROSCOE CONKLING.
MWA, NBuG, NNUW.

g) Weed, Parsons & Co., Albany, N. Y., 1889, 53p.
PROCEEDINGS OF THE SENATE AND ASSEMBLY
OF THE STATE OF NEW YORK IN RELATION
TO THE DEATH OF EX-SENATOR ROSCOE
CONKLING.
DLC.

85 THE TRUTH (DE 4:71-111)

a) C. P. Farrell, New York, 1897, 52p.
DLC, NBuG, NN, NcU.

*b) Banner of Light, Boston, [c1899].

*c) Peter Eckler, New York, [c1899].

d) Pioneer Press, London, [19—], 15p. THE TRUTH
ABOUT THE CHURCH.

e) Haldeman-Julius, Girard, Kansas, n.d., 36p. THE
TRUTH and GHOSTS.

86 THE TRUTH OF HISTORY [From *Truth Seeker*, 1887]
(DE 11:391-395)

a) [Truth Seeker Co., New York, 1887], 7p.
NN.

*b) C. P. Farrell, New York, [c1903].

87 VINDICATION OF THOMAS PAINE [In reply to the Utica, New York, *Observer*] (DE 5:447-524)

  a) I. N. Choynski, San Francisco, 1877, 39p.
    CU, CtY, ViU.

  b) J. P. Mendum, Boston, 1877, 35p.
    CtY, DLC, NN, OCHi, PU.

  c) Saturday Evening Call, Peoria, Illinois, 1877, 35p.
    DLC, NcD.

  d) Truth Seeker Co., New York, 1887, 76p. [Also contains "A Roman Catholic Canard."]
    NN.

 *e) Banner of Light, Boston, [c1899].

 *f) Peter Eckler, New York, [c1903].

  g) C. P. Farrell, New York, [c1903], 78p. [Pages numbered 447-524.]
    NN.

  h) Baldwin's Bookstore, Chicago, [1880], 9p. COL. ROBERT G. INGERSOLL'S VINDICATION OF THOMAS PAINE.
    CSmH, CtY.

  i) Thomas Williams, Chicago, [c1900]. COL. ROBERT G. INGERSOLL'S VINDICATION OF THOMAS PAINE.

  j) Truth Seeker Co., New York, n.d., 40p. THOMAS PAINE'S VINDICATION. ["Truth Seeker Tract #123."]
    CSmH, CtY.

  k) Haldeman-Julius, Girard, Kansas, [1920], 64p. ["Little Blue Book #88."]

88 VOLTAIRE (DE 3:177-248)

  a) C. P. Farrell, New York, 1895, 74p.
    DLC, NN, OHi, WaU.

 *b) Banner of Light, Boston, [c1899].

*c) Peter Eckler, New York, [c1899].
  d) R. Forder, London, 1892, 32p. ORATION ON
     VOLTAIRE.
     ICN, MH, NN.
  e) Freethought Publishing Co., London, [c1895].
     ORATION ON VOLTAIRE.

89 WHAT IS RELIGION? (DE 4:479-508)

  a) Freethought Publishing Co., London, [c1895], 16p.
     NN.
  b) Boston Investigator Co., Boston, 1899, 19p.
 *c) J. S. Ogilvie, New York, 1928.
  d) Pioneer Press, London, [19—], 16p.
 *e) C. P. Farrell, New York, 1899. PROGRESS and
     WHAT IS RELIGION?
  f) R. Forder, London, 1899, 16p. PROGRESS and WHAT
     IS RELIGION?
     ICN.
  g) Truth Seeker Co., New York, 1899, 21p. PROGRESS
     and WHAT IS RELIGION? ["Truth Seeker Tracts
     ns #39." Also contains "Declaration of the Free."]
     NN, NcD.

90 WHAT MUST WE DO TO BE SAVED? (DE 1:441-525)

  a) C. P. Farrell, Washington, D. C., 1880, 89p.
     DLC, EBM, OHi.
  b) [Abel Heywood & Son, Manchester, England], 1881,
     112p. ["Leek Bijou Freethought Reprints,"]
     EBM.
  c) Freethought Publishing Co., London, 1884, 2 parts.
     [A 1902 ed. was in 1 part, 39p.]
     EBM.

d) C. P. Farrell, New York, 1889, 88p.
DLC, IU, MB, NN, ViU.

*e) Banner of Light, Boston, [c1899].

*f) Peter Eckler, New York, [c1899].

*g) Truth Seeker Co., New York, [c1899].

*h) J. S. Ogilvie, New York, 1928.

i) Haldeman-Julius, Girard, Kansas, [1949?], 24p. [Also contains 6 short tributes in 8p.]

j) John Barres, Josiah Gimson, Michael Wright, Philip Wright & W. Larner Sugden, Leek, England, 1881, 80p. WHAT MUST I DO TO BE SAVED?
[Later editions have 88p.]
EBM.

k) Watts & Co., London, 1881, 88p. WHAT MUST I DO TO BE SAVED?
NN.

l) W. H. Morrish, Bristol, [England], n.d., WHAT MUST I DO TO BE SAVED?

m) Truth Seeker Co., New York, 1882. INGERSOLL'S CREED. ["Truth Seeker Tract #163." Epigrams from WMWDTBS.]

n) n.p., n. place, [188-], 8p. COL. INGERSOLL'S GREAT LECTURE ON "WMWDTBS" AND HIS VIEWS ON POLITICS AND RELIGION.
DLC.

91 WHAT WOULD YOU SUBSTITUTE FOR THE BIBLE AS A MORAL GUIDE? (DE 11:537-544)

a) Truth Seeker Co., New York, [c1899], 9p. BIBLE NOT A MORAL GUIDE. ["Truth Seeker Tracts ns #28."]

*b) C. P. Farrell, New York, [c1903]. BIBLE NOT A MORAL GUIDE.

92 WHICH WAY? (DE 3:339-449)

 a) C. P. Farrell, New York, 1895, 53p.
 NN, NNUW.
 b) Freethought Publishing Co., London, 1885, 16p.
 [Pages numbered 273-288. "2nd Ed."]
 c) J. P. Mendum, Boston, 1885, 14p.
 *d) Peter Eckler, New York, [c1899].
 *e) Truth Seeker Co., New York, [c1899].
 f) Haldeman-Julius, Girard, Kansas, [1948?], 17p.
 WHICH WAY TO A FREE WORLD?

93 WHY AM I AN AGNOSTIC? [From *NAR*, 1890]
 (DE 11:237-259)

 a) Progressive Publishing Co., London, 1890, 2 parts.
 NcD.
 *b) Banner of Light, Boston, [c1899].
 *c) Peter Eckler, New York, [c1899].
 d) Freethought Publishing Co., London, 1902, 23p.
 [Also issued in 2 parts.]
 EBM, NN.
 e) Watts & Co., London, 1912, 2 parts, 15 & 24p.
 ICN, NN.

94 WHY COL. INGERSOLL OPPOSES THE DEMOCRATS
 [From "Indianapolis Speech, 1876."] (DE 9:157-187)

 a) n.p., n. place, [1870?]. [Broadside.]
 DLC.
 b) n.p., n. place, n.d., 4p. ARRAIGNMENT OF THE
 DEMOCRATIC PARTY.
 OClWHi.

95 WHY I AM AN AGNOSTIC (DE 4:5-67)

 a) C. P. Farrell, New York, 1897, 84p.
 DLC, NN, OC.

96 A WOODEN GOD [From the Chicago *Times*, March 27, 1880] (DE 11:143-166)

   a) C. P. Farrell, New York, 1889, 88p.
     DLC, IU, MB, NN, ViU.
   b) Freethought Publishing Co., London, 1903, 14p.
     EBM.

II. Works with Contributions by Ingersoll

Arranged Alphabetically by Title.

97 *Agnosticism and Other Essays* by Edgar Fawcett. Chicago: Belford, Clarke and Co., 1889, 227p. [Prologue by RGI.] (DE 12:55-65) DLC, NN, OCU, PP.

98 *An American Bible* edited by Alice Hubbard. East Aurora, N. Y.: Roycrofters, 1911. [RGI on pages 185-216.] OC, OCl, OT.

99 *Arsenal for Skeptics* by Richard W. Hinton [pseud. of Charles Angoff].

a) New York: Alfred A. Knopf, 1934, 372p. [RGI's "What is Religion?" is on pages 316-323.]
b) New York: A. S. Barnes Co., 1961, 372p. [RGI's "What is Religion?" is on pages 316-323.]

100 *At the Graveside of Walt Whitman: Harleigh, Camden, N. J., March 30th and Sprigs of Lilac . . . 1892*, edited by Horace Traubel. Philadelphia: Billstein & Son, 1892. [RGI's speech on pages 18-22.] OU.

101 *The Brain and the Bible; Or the Conflict Between Mental Science and Theology* by Edgar C. Beall. Cincinnati: Author, 1882, 263p. [Preface by RGI page vii-xxii.] (DE 12:27-35)
DLC, OC, OCHi, NN.

102 *Col. Ingersoll's Decoration Day Address, May 30, 1888.* New York: M. J. Ivers & Co., 1888, 26p. [Also contains Decoration Day Speeches of C. M. Depew & Col. Black.]

103 *Elbert Hubbard's Scrap Book.* New York: William H. Wise Publishers, 1923. [Contains ten RGI selections.]

104 *Faith or Fact* ... by Henry M. Taber. New York: Peter Eckler, 1897, 331p. [Preface by RGI.] (DE 12:69-77)
EBM, NN, OC, OO.

105* *For Her Daily Bread* by "Litere" [pseud. of Lillian E. Sommers.] Chicago: Rand McNally & Co., 1887. [Preface by RGI.] (DE 12: 47-52)
[DLC]

106 *Great Republican Speeches of the Campaign of 1881.* New York: Staten Island Publishing Co., 1881, 72p.
OFH.

107 *Has Freethought a Constructive Side?* (DE 11:437-442)
    *a) New York: C. P. Farrell, [c1903].
    b) [New York]: Exit Enterprises, 1968, 6p. [Offset of 1890 *Truth Seeker* art. See #220.]
    c) New York: Truth Seeker Co., 1890, 82p. *Freethought, Is It Constructive or Destructive?* [RGI on pages 3-10]
    DLC.

108 *I Died* by Charles Collis. New York: The Irving Press,
1926, 186p. [Correspondence with RGI on Lincoln's
religion.]
DLC, NN.

109 *Infidels and Heretics* by Clarence Darrow and Wallace Rice.
Boston: Stratford Co., 1929. [Excerpts from RGI
pages 22-23, 113-114, 125-128, 223-224, 235, 245-246.]
OU.

110* *Is Divorce Wrong?* by Robert G. Ingersoll, Cardinal
James Gibbons, and Rev. Henry C. Potter. New York:
C. P. Farrell, [c1902].

111 *Liberty of Man, Woman and Child* plus *Little Journey
to the Home of Robert G. Ingersoll* by Robert G. Ingersoll
and Elbert Hubbard, respectively. East Aurora, N. Y.:
Roycrofters, 1924, 111p.
OC.

112 *Life and Writings of Thomas Paine* edited by D. E.
Wheeler. New York: V. Parke & Co., 1908, 10 vols.
[Vol. I contains RGI's essay on Paine.]
NN, OU.

113 *Lord's Day or Man's?* by Byron Sunderland & W. A.
Croffut. [New York: Truth Seeker Co., 1899], 152p.
[Preface by RGI.] (Not in DE)
DLC, NNUT, NcU, RPB.

114 *Men, Women and Gods and Other Lectures* by Helen H.
Gardener. New York: Truth Seeker Co., 1885, 158p.
[Introduction by RGI.]
EBM, MiD, NN, OCo.

115 *Mistakes of Ingersoll, and His Answers Complete* edited by
J. B. McClure. Chicago: Rhodes & McClure, 1880, 151p.
[Contains RGI's "Mistakes of Moses," "Skulls,"
"WMWDTBS," and "Thomas Paine," in "unauthorized"
versions.]
EBM, MB, NcD, OO.

116 *Modern Thinkers* by Van Buren Denslow. Chicago:
Belford Clarke & Co., 1880. [Introduction by RGI,
pages xi-xxxii.] (DE 12:7-23)
CtY, DLC, EBM, ICJ, ICRL, MiU, NN, OD, OO.

117 *Napoleon* by Charles Phillips. Brooklyn, N. Y.: Brewster
Publishers, 1924, 13p. [Limited to 234 copies. One
of the four essays is by RGI.]
DLC, NN.

118* *Our Political Degradation*, by Hawkins. New York:
[n.p. ?] 1904. [Contains "Is Avarice Triumphant?"
pages 196-219.]
MB.

119 *Pen Portrait of James G. Blaine* by Henry J. Ramsdell.
[Columbus, Ohio?]: n.p., 1876, 8p. [Contains speech by
RGI.]
DLC.

120 *The Philosophy of Shakespeare* by Anderson M. Baten.
Kingsport, Tenn.: Kingsport Press, 1937, 596p.
["Book two" is by RGI.]
OC.

121 *Proceedings of the Civil Rights Mass-Meeting . . .
Speeches of F. Douglass and Robert G. Ingersoll.*
Washington, D. C.: C. P. Farrell, 1883. 53p.

[RGI on pages 15-53.]
EBM, OCHi.

122 *The Religion of Lincoln: Correspondence between Collis and Ingersoll.* New York: G. W. Dillingham, [1901?], 24p.
DLC, EBM, OCo, OClWHi.

123 *Republican Club, City of New York, Addresses.* [New York]: n.p., 1909. [Contains RGI's "Abraham Lincoln." pages 69-78.]
MB.

124 *Robert G. Ingersoll, Gen. Wm. T. Sherman, Chauncey M. Depew, Their Speeches at the Robson & Crane Banquet.* [New York]: [n.p.?], [1887?], 15p.
DLC, MB, MH, ViU.

125 *Vindication of Thomas Paine* by Robert G. Ingersoll and *Thomas Paine, A Criticism* by Moncure D. Conway. Chicago: Belford Clarke & Co., 1879, 55p.
DLC, N, NN.

126 *Voices in Dissent* edited by Arthur A. Ekrich, Jr. New York: Citadel Press, 1964, 381p. [RGI's "What is Religion?" is on pages 187-194.]
DLC, IaAS, MB, MH, NN, NjR, OCU, OrCS.

127 *Wit, Wisdom and Eloquence* compiled by Randal Lockhart Gray. Atlanta: Harrison Co., 1930, 443p. [Majority of Selections by RGI.]
MiD.

128 *The Women of the Bible* by Robert G. Ingersoll, with *A Sketch of Colonel Ingersoll* by Charles Watts. London:

Watts & Co., [c1895], 16p. [RGI's contribution is from the later part of the "Third Interview on Talmage."] (DE 5:111-114)

III. Ingersoll's Contributions to Periodicals

1874

129 "Extracts from a Discourse on Heretics and Heresies,"
Truth Seeker 1(12):10-12.

130 "Oration on the Gods," *Truth Seeker* 1(9):10-11,
1(10):10-11, 1(11):10-11.

131 "Arraignment of the Church and a Plea for Individuality,"
Truth Seeker 2(1):10-11, 2(2):10-11.

1875

132 "An Oration on Thomas Paine," *Truth Seeker* 2(22):6-7,
10-11.

133 "Oration on Humboldt," *Truth Seeker* 2(23):6-7.

1877

134 "Ghosts," *Truth Seeker* 4:106-107. [Excerpt of lecture.]

135 "Liberty for Man, Woman and Child," *Truth Seeker*
4:236-238.

136 "Colonel Ingersoll's Review of his Reviewers,"
Truth Seeker 4:314-315, 322-323.

137 "Paine Vindicated," *Truth Seeker* 4:331-332, 338-340.

1878

138 "Ghosts," *Truth Seeker* 5:68-72. [Page 72 misnumbered "66".]

139 "Thomas Paine Glorified," *Truth Seeker* 5:82-85.

140 "Hell," *Truth Seeker* 5:98-101.

1879

141 "Mistakes of Moses." *Truth Seeker* 6:290-293.

142 "Ebon C. Ingersoll's Funeral," *Truth Seeker* 6:361.

143 "Letter from Robert G. Ingersoll," *Truth Seeker* 6:589. [On obscenity in the mails.]

144 "Ingersoll Interviewed," *Truth Seeker* 6:605. [From the Cincinnati *Gazette*.]

145 "An Extract from Ingersoll's 'Some Mistakes of Moses,' " *Truth Seeker* 6:762.

1880

146 "Ingersoll on Shakespeare and the Stage," *Truth Seeker* 7:459. [A letter.]

147 "Col. Ingersoll on the Political Situation," *Truth Seeker* 7:459. [A letter.]

148 "Hell," *Truth Seeker* 7:370-371. [From the Cincinnati *Commercial*.]

149 "Stories as Told by Colonel Ingersoll," *Truth Seeker* 7:26.

1881

150 "Ingersoll's Creed," *Truth Seeker* 8:7. [Epigrams from "WMWDTBS."]

151 "Colonel Ingersoll Talks about his Threatened Indictment in Delaware for Blasphemy," *Truth Seeker* 8:170-171.

152 "The Christian Religion," *NAR* 133:109-152, 477-522. [Ingersoll-Black Debate. The first half of part I was written by RGI; while the second half was written by Jeremiah S. Black, who was Secretary of State under President Buchanan. Part II was entirely RGI's; Black declined an invitation to respond. Professor George P. Fisher of Yale answered, without referring to RGI by name, in the February 1882 *NAR*.]

1882

153 "To the Indianapolis Clergy," *The Iconclast* (Indianapolis), Jan. 1882. [RGI's reply to clerical statements printed in Indianapolis papers following his visit.] (DE 7:125-167)

154 "Colonel Ingersoll and the Rev. Mr. Talmage," *Truth Seeker* 9:72-73. [An interview.]

155 "Colonel Ingersoll's Decoration Day Oration," *Truth Seeker* 9:361.

156 "Ingersoll's Interviews on Talmage," *Truth Seeker* 9:376-377. [A book review with extensive quotes.]

1883

157 "Col. Ingersoll Makes the Clergy Appear Small,"
Truth Seeker 10:298-299. [An interview from the Chicago
Daily News.]

158 "Col. Ingersoll on the Situation," *Truth Seeker* 10:500-501.
[An interview from the Brooklyn *Union.*]

159 "Colonel Ingersoll Defends Mr. Holyoake," *Truth Seeker*
10:519. [A letter from the Boston *Investigator.*]

160 "Further Views of Col. Ingersoll on the Situation,"
Truth Seeker 10:530-531. [An interview from the
Brooklyn *Union.*]

161 "Colonel Ingersoll's Opinions," *Truth Seeker*
10:692-693. [An interview.]

1884

162 "A New Lecture by Colonel Ingersoll," *Truth Seeker*
11:210-213. ["Orthodoxy." Repeated *Truth Seeker*
11:258-261.]

163 "Colonel Ingersoll Catechised," *Truth Seeker* 11:674-675.
[An interview from the *San Franciscan* of Oct. 4, 1884.]

1885

164 "Inspiration," *Truth Seeker Annual* (1885), 45-48.
(DE 11:383-387)

165 "Which Way?" *Truth Seeker* 12:34-35, 38.

166 "Blasphemy," *Truth Seeker* 12:146-147. [An abridged
version.]

167 "A Few Remarks by Colonel Ingersoll," *Truth Seeker* 12:294-295. [Address to the Ingersoll Secular Society, Boston, April 19, 1885.]

168 "Colonel Ingersoll on the Revision," *Truth Seeker* 12:498-499. [An interview from the Boston *Evening Record.*]

169 "Colonel Ingersoll's Ideas upon Some Live Topics," *Truth Seeker* 12:564-565. [Initial publication.]

170 "American Secular Union Congress," *Truth Seeker* 12:681, 684. ["Myth and Miracle."]

171 "Introduction to Men, Women and Gods," *Truth Seeker* 12:706.

1886

172 "Elizur Wright," *NAR* 142:209-211. [A tribute to the memory of the dead reformer.] (DE 12:409-412).

173* "A Lay Sermon," *Truth Seeker* 13: (Nov. 1886). (DE 4:211-235)

1887

174* "The Truth of History," *Truth Seeker* 14: (Feb. 19, 1887). (DE 11:391-395).

175 "Some Interrogation Points," *NAR* 144:217-230. [On economics and politics.] (DE 11:191-199)

176 "The McGlynn Case," *The Independent Pulpit* (Waco, Texas) 5:52-54. [From the Brooklyn *Times.* The version

appearing in DE 8:284-291 comes from the Brooklyn *Citizen*, April, 1886.]

177 "Secularism," *The Independent Pulpit* 5:113. (DE 11:405-406)

178 "A Reply to the Rev. Henry M. Field, D.D.," *NAR* 145:473-505. [For Field's articles see *NAR* 145:128-145; 616-628.] (DE 6:121-218) See #182.

179 "Tribute to Henry Ward Beecher," *Truth Seeker* 14:420.

180 "Trial for Blasphemy," *Truth Seeker* 14:344-345.

181 "Blasphemy," *Truth Seeker* 14:55.

1888

182 "Letter to Dr. Field," *NAR* 146:31-46. [RGI-Field debate.] See #178.

183 "Art and Morality," *NAR* 146:318-326. (DE 11:203-211)

184 "Colonel Ingersoll to Mr. Gladstone," *NAR* 146:601-640. [RGI-Gladstone debate. For William E. Gladstone's challenge see *NAR* 146:481-508.]

185 "The Divided Household of Faith," *NAR* 147:150-164. (DE 11:215-233)

186 "Rome or Reason?: A Reply to Cardinal Manning," *NAR* 147:394-414, 502-524. [For Henry Edward Manning's challenge see *NAR* 147:241-269. He was Cardinal of Westminster and England's leading Catholic.]

187 "Stage and Pulpit," *Truth Seeker*, 15:18-19.
(DE 8:296-306)

188 "Colonel Ingersoll to Mr. Gladstone," *Freethought*
(San Francisco) 1:289-291. [An abridged version from
NAR.]

189 "Ingersoll's Views on Oratory," *Freethought* 1:303-304.
[From *The Examiner.*]

190 "A Beautiful Tribute," *Freethought* 1:402-403.
[RGI at funeral of Courtlandt Palmer.]

191 "Ingersoll's Reply to Cardinal Manning," *Freethought*
1:523-525, 537-538, 560-561, 570-571, 583-584, 608-609,
620-621, 2:12-13(1889). [From *NAR.*]

192 "Colonel Ingersoll's Letter to Dr. Field," *Freethought*
1:17-20. [Abridged from *NAR.*]

193 "The Stage and the Pulpit," *Freethought* 1:45. [From
the *Truth Seeker.*]

194 "Art and Morality," *Freethought* 1:128-129. [From
NAR.]

195 "Ingersoll's Tribute to Conkling," *Freethought* 1:242-243.

1889

196 "A Tribute to Horace Seaver," Boston *Investigator*
(August 28, 1889), 6. [Written upon the death of the
editor of that publication.] (DE 12:459-466)

197 "Professor Huxley and Agnosticism," *NAR* 148:403-416.

198 "Is Divorce Wrong," *NAR* 149:513-538. [Discussion by
Samuel W. Dike, James Cardinal Gibbons, Henry C. Potter,
and RGI. RGI's contribution, in the form of answers
to questions, is found on pages 529-538.] (DE 6:397-429)

199 "Why Am I an Agnostic?" *NAR* 149:741-749. [Part I]
(DE 11:237-259) See #204.

200 "Professor Huxley and Agnosticism," *Freethought*
2:233-234, 248-249. [From *NAR*.]

201 "Liberalism, a Symposium," *Truth Seeker Annual* (1889),
28-31. [RGI's part.]

202 "Horace Seaver," *Freethought* 2:583-586. [From
Boston *Investigator*.]

203 "Is Divorce Wrong?" *Freethought* 2:730-731, 744-745.
[From *NAR*.]

1890

204 "Why Am I an Agnostic?" *NAR* 150:330-338.
[Part II.] See #199.

205 "God in the Constitution," *The Arena* 1:119-130. [Written
in response to the growing movement to amend the
preamble to the Constitution by inserting references to
God. Bishop Spalding replied to RGI in *The Arena* at
1:517-528.] (DE 11:121-134)

206 "Tolstoi and 'The Kreutzer Sonata,'" *NAR* 151:289-299.
[A criticism of Tolstoi's book, and a plea that its
banishment from the U. S. mails be ended.]
(DE 11:305-318)

207 "Ingersoll on Christmas," *Freethought* 3:40. [From the New York *Tribune*.]

208 "Why I Am an Agnostic," *Freethought* 3:201-202. [Abridged from *NAR*.]

209 "Ingersoll on Labor," *Freethought* 3:298. [From the New York *Morning Journal*.]

210 "Giordano Bruno," *Freethinker's Magazine* (Buffalo) 7:477-480.

211 "Mary Hewins Fiske—An Obituary Address," *Freethinker's Magazine* 7:109-110.

212 "The Gospel of Humanity," *Freethinker's Magazine* 7:11-18. [An interview from the New York *World*.]

213 "Horace Seaver," *Freethinker's Magazine* 7:429-435.

214 "Ingersoll on Tolstoi," *Freethought* 3:583. [From the *NAR*.]

215 "Testimonial to Walt Whitman," *Freethought* 3:728-730. [From the *Truth Seeker*.]

216 "God in the Constitution," *Freethinker's Magazine* 8:564-574. [From *The Arena*.]

217 "Is There a Tomorrow for the Human Race?" *Light* (London) 10:468. [From RGI's speech at the Lotos Club, New York, March 22, 1890.] (DE 12:113-114)

218 "Crumbling Creeds," *The Twentieth Century* (New York), April 24, 1890. (DE 11:463-470)

219 "Crimes Against Criminals," *Truth Seeker* 17:67-69.

220 "Freethought—Destructive, Constructive or Both?"
Truth Seeker 17:82. [RGI's part of a discussion.]
(DE 11:437-442)

221 (A letter), *Truth Seeker* 17:357. [Praises the platform of
the Women's Liberal Union.]

222 "Ingersoll on Oratory," *Truth Seeker* 17:406-407.
["From the Philadelphia *Press*."]

223 "Ingersoll on Vivisection," *Truth Seeker* 17:419.
[From the St. Louis *Globe Democrat*.]

224 "Tolstoi and 'The Kreutzer Sonata,' " *Truth Seeker*
17:580-581 [Excerpts from *NAR*.] See #206.

225 "Our Schools," *Truth Seeker* 17:599. [From *The World*,
Sept. 7, 1890.]

226 "Colonel Ingersoll on Sunday Observance," *Truth Seeker*
17:615. [An interview from the New York *Morning
Journal*.]

227 "Testimonial to Walt Whitman," *Truth Seeker*
17:690-693, 700. [This is the first appearance in print
of what would later be called "Liberty in Literature."
The actual lecture was given in Camden, N. J., only eleven
days earlier.] (DE 3:249-304)

1891

228 "Colonel Ingersoll Speaks of the Tendency of Modern
Thought and Other Things," *Truth Seeker* 18:724-725.
[From the Chicago *Tribune*.]

229 "The Three Philanthropists," *Truth Seeker* 18:770. [Abridged from *NAR.*]

230 "Colonel Ingersoll on Liberty," *Truth Seeker* 18:786-787, 790. ["LMWC." From the Chicago *Tribune.*]

231 "Spirituality," *The Conservator* (Philadelphia), 1:18. (DE 11:481-485)

232* "A Word about Education," *The High School Register* (Omaha) Jan. 1891. [The existence of this publication is unverified. This reference is found in DE 11:369-371.]

233 "Is Avarice Triumphant?" *NAR* 152:671-681. (DE 7:427-447)

234 "The Three Philanthropists," *NAR* 153:661-671. (DE 11:343-353)

235 "Effect of the World's Fair on the Human Race," *Halligan's Illustrated World's Fair* (December 1891), 4. (DE 12:361-365)

1892

236 "Colonel Ingersoll Quashes Dr. Buckley," *Truth Seeker* 19:21. [Christmas sermon.]

237 "Colonel Ingersoll to the Rev. Mr. King," *Truth Seeker* 19:39-41. [A letter from the New York *Evening Telegram.*]

238 "Ingersoll to the Unitarian Association," *Truth Seeker* 19:56-57.

239 "Plays and Players," *Truth Seeker* 19:71-72. [An interview from the New York *Dramatic Mirror.*]

240 "Mr. Ingersoll on Walt Whitman," *Light* 12:201. [An incomplete printing of Ingersoll's speech at Whitman's funeral.] (DE 12:473-477)

241 "Ernest Renan," *NAR* 155:608-622. (DE 11:283-301)

242 "The Church of the Future," *Freethinker's Magazine* 10:13-15.

243 "Unitarianism—Character for Creed," *Freethinker's Magazine* 10:144-156. [Address before the New York Unitarian Club.]

244 "Thomas Paine," *Freethinker's Magazine* 10:213-222. [Address at the Manhattan Liberal Club, January 29, 1892.]

245 "Address at the Funeral of Walt Whitman," *Freethinker's Magazine* 10:267-270.

246 "The Paine Anniversary," *Truth Seeker* 19:88-89. [RGI's speech.]

247 "Ingersoll's Final Reply to his *Telegram* Critics," *Truth Seeker* 19:100-101, 104-105, 108. [A letter from the New York *Evening Telegram*.]

1893

248 "Should the Chinese be Excluded?" *NAR* 157:52-58. [The last two pages are by Rep. Thomas J. Geary of California; prompted by the passage of the Chinese Exclusion Law of 1892.] (DE 11:357-365)

249 "Colonel Ingersoll on Progress," *Truth Seeker* 20:9. [Abridged version of RGI's previously unpublished, first public lecture.]

1894

250 "Thomas Paine," *NAR* 155:181-195. [This is only one of RGI's several pieces with a similar title.] (DE 11:321-339)

251 "Ingersoll's Tribute to Thomas Paine," *Truth Seeker* 21:358-359.

252 "Ingersoll on Suicide," *Truth Seeker* 21:519-520.

253 "Ingersoll and his Critics," *Truth Seeker* 21:598-599. [On suicide.]

254 "Ingersoll's Views on Religion," *Truth Seeker* 21:614-615. [An interview from the New York *Herald.*]

255 "Ingersoll on Brockway," *Truth Seeker* 21:632. [From the New York *World.*]

256 "Is Suicide a Sin?" *Freethinker's Magazine* 12:488-494. [From the New York *World.*]

1895

257 "Ingersoll in New York," *Truth Seeker* 22:742-743. [Excerpts from "Foundations of Faith."]

258 "Personal Experiences of Two American Anti-Vivisectionists in Various Countries," by Philip G. Peabody, *New England Anti-Vivisection Society Quarterly,* 1(1):1-96. [Appendix also by RGI.]

1896

259 "Ingersoll on Money," *Truth Seeker* 23:633. [A letter.]

1897

260 "Ingersoll on 'The Truth,' " *Truth Seeker* 24:246-247.

261 "Colonel Ingersoll's Latest," *Truth Seeker* 24:725, 728-729.
[Extracts from "Why I Am an Agnostic."]

262 "What I Want for Christmas," *The Arena* 18:721-722.
[Part of a larger article entitled "Idylls and Ideals
of Christmas."] (DE 11:375-376)

263 "What I Want for Christmas," *Truth Seeker* 24:824.
[From *The Arena.*]

1898

264 "A Look Backward and a Prophecy," *Truth Seeker*
25:550-551. [25th anniversary issue. It was reprinted
in the 50th anniversary issue (Sept. 1, 1923), 571-572.]
(DE 11:563-576)

265 "Colonel Ingersoll on the Dismals," *Light* 18:424. [This
article on depression seems to have never appeared
elsewhere.]

266 "Ingersoll on Spain and Cuba," *Truth Seeker* 24:326-327.
[From a speech at McVicar's Theater, May 1, 1898.]

267 "Ingersoll on Superstition," *Truth Seeker* 25:694-696.
[Initial publication.]

1899

268 "Faith That Surely Wanes," *Truth Seeker* 26:294-295.
[Initial publication.]

269 "Ingersoll's Paine Oration," *Truth Seeker* 26:326-329, 332. ["Why We Honor Thomas Paine."]

270 "Declaration of the Free," *Truth Seeker* 26:341.

271 "The Agnostic's Side," *NAR* 169:289-321. [A reprint of "A Reply to the Rev. Henry M. Field, D.D.," *NAR* (1887) 145:473-505. It was probably reprinted as a tribute to RGI upon his death.]

272 "Ingersoll Interviewed," by John Emery McLean, Ed., *Mind* (New York) 3(6):321-328.

273 "The Glories of This Century," *Truth Seeker* 26:199-200. [Speech.]

274 "A Tribute by Ingersoll," *Truth Seeker* 26:216-217. [At the funeral of Isaac H. Bailey.]

275 "Reviewed by Colonel Ingersoll," *Truth Seeker* 26:358-359. [An interview by Rev. Briggs. From the New York *World.*]

276 "Col. Ingersoll on Religion," *Truth Seeker* 26:407-409. [From the Boston *Investigator.*]

277 "The Custom of Oath-Taking," *Truth Seeker* 26:422-423. [An interview with C. Watts.]

278 "Declaration of the Free," *Free Thought Magazine* (Chicago) 17:365-368.

279 "Thomas Paine," *Free Thought Magazine* 17:609-618.

280 "The Old and the New," *The Torch of Reason* (Silverton, Oregon) 2:1 (February 2, 1899). [From the *Truth Seeker Annual* (1899).]

281 "The Declaration of the Free," *The Torch of Reason*
   3(32):1.

IV. Collected Essays and Works by Ingersoll

282 THE WORKS OF ROBERT G. INGERSOLL.

a) DRESDEN EDITION. C. P. Farrell, New York, 1900.
[Reprinted in 1902, 1909-11, 1912, 1915. In 12 volumes
prior to 1911, after which a 13th volume, INGERSOLL:
A BIOGRAPHICAL APPRECIATION by Herman
Kittredge, was added. The 12 volumes are arranged
as follows: Volumes 1-4, LECTURES; Volumes 5-7,
DISCUSSIONS; Volume 8, INTERVIEWS; Volume 9,
POLITICAL; Volume 10, LEGAL; Volumes 11-12,
MISCELLANY; Volume 13, BIOGRAPHY. Volume 12
contains a 122p. index compiled by G. E. Macdonald
of the *Truth Seeker*, which is extensive if not always
accurate. The editor of the DE tried to include everything
published by RGI, and a good number of unpublished
things, too. Also included are many of the press
interviews granted by RGI for which many of the
newspaper names and dates are incomplete or inaccurate
because the editor used the Ingersoll family collection
of clippings. The DE must, however, remain the
definitive edition of RGI's work for the present. C. P.
Farrell published many of the original editions of RGI's
single works; apparently the same plates were used
for those sections of the DE.]
CU, DLC, InU, LU, MB, MH, MiU, O, OCl, OClW, OCU,

61

OD, OT, OU, NN, PHC, PP, RPB, TV, TxU, Vi.
b) EDITION DE LUXE. National Library Company, New
York, 1910. [In 5 volumes. Limited to 1000 sets. Edited,
with biography and notes by Jennie Ellis Burdick.
The text is not from the DE, but rather seems to have come
from the stenographical transcriptions of RGI's lectures
found in many of the "Complete Lectures of Col.
RGI" books. See #288.]
DLC.
c) CENTENARY EDITION. The Ingersoll League, New
York, 1929. [Reprinted in 1933. Apparently from DE
plates. In 12 volumes.]
DLC, LU, ViU.
d) THE NEW DRESDEN EDITION. The Ingersoll
Publishers, New York, [c1930]. [Apparently DE plates.
In 12 volumes.]
DLC, NN, PU, ViU.

283 COL. INGERSOLL'S AMERICAN SECULAR
LECTURES. Heywood & Son, Manchester, England,
1882. [Only 12 parts were published.]
EBM.

284 COL. R. G. INGERSOLL'S FAMOUS SPEECHES
COMPLETE.
a) L. Lipkind, New York, 1906, 354 p. [Issued in
both cloth and paperbound forms.]
MH, OCl, PP.
b) Monarch Book Co., Chicago, 1906, 354 p.
CtY, NN.

285 COL. ROBERT G. INGERSOLL'S 44 COMPLETE
LECTURES. M. A. Donohue, Chicago, 1924, 411p.
MB, NN, OC, OCl, OD.

286 COL. INGERSOLL'S THREE GREAT SPEECHES.
Rhodes & McClure, Chicago, 1881, 64p. [Contains "To the
Farmers of Illinois," "To the Veteran Soldiers,"
"To the American Citizens."]
DLC, OHi.

287* COL. R. INGERSOLL'S LECTURES. n.p., [Chicago,
1879-80?], No. 1-24. ["13 volumes in one."]
ICN.

288 COMPLETE LECTURES OF COL. R. G. INGERSOLL.

a) Baldwin's Bookstore, Chicago, [1880], various pagings.
DLC.
b) n.p., n. place, [c1880], 408p. ["Published for the
Trade."]
CU, ICJ, ICRL, IU, LU, MnU, NN.
*c) Banner of Light, Boston, [c1899].
*d) C. P. Farrell, New York, [c1899]. [Identical to #325?]
*e) Peter Eckler, New York, [c1899].
*f) Rhodes, Chicago, [c1899].
*g) J. Regan & Co., Chicago, [191-].
h) M. A. Donohue & Co., Chicago, [191-], 411p.
CU, DLC, FTaSU, ViU.
i) Regan Publishing Co., Chicago, 1926, 411p.
j) David McKay Co., Philadelphia, [1935], 411p.
DLC, NN, TxDaM.

289 DEBATES WITH THE CLERGY. Haldeman-Jullius,
Girard, Kansas. [192-], 47p. [Contains: "My Chicago Bible
Class," "To the Indianapolis Clergy," "To the Brooklyn
Divines," "The Limitations of Toleration."]
KU.

290 THE ENEMIES OF INDIVIDUALITY AND MENTAL FREEDOM. Haldeman-Julius, Girard, Kansas, n.d., 32p. [Contains the title selection plus 7 short pieces.]

291 ESSAYS AND CRITICISMS.

a) C. P. Farrell, New York, 1897, 77p. [Contains "Why Am I an Agnostic?" "Huxley and Agnosticism," "Ernest Renan," and "Count Tolstoi and 'The Kreutzer Sonata.' "]
DLC.
*b) Banner of Light, Boston, [c1899].
*c) Peter Eckler, New York, [c1899].
*d) Truth Seeker Co., New York, [c1899].
e) Haldeman-Julius, Girard, Kansas, n.d., 39p. ESSAYS BY AN AGNOSTIC AND CRITICISMS BY A SKEPTIC. [Same contents as a) above)

292 FIFTY GREAT SELECTIONS, LECTURES, TRIBUTES, AFTER DINNER SPEECHES AND ESSAYS . . . . C. P. Farrell, New York, 1920, various pagings. [Apparently from DE plates.]
DLC, NN, OCl, OT, TxU.

293* FORTY-FOUR LECTURES. Stein Publishing Co., Chicago, [c1902].

294 FRAGMENTS AND RANDOM THOUGHTS. Haldeman-Julius, Girard, Kansas, n.d., 31p. [Text from DE. Includes "Reply to Dr. Lyman Abbott" and "Effects of the World's Fair on the Human Race."]
KU.

295 THE GHOSTS AND OTHER LECTURES.

a) C. P. Farrell, Peoria, Illinois, 1878, 232 p. [First collected edition. Contains "Ghosts," "LMWC," "About

Farming . . . ," "Declaration of Independence," "Speech at
Cincinnati," "Past Rises Before Me Like a Dream."
CLSU, DLC, MB, MoU, ViU.

b) C. P. Farrell, Washington, D. C., 1878, 232p. [Same
as above except for title page.]
CtY, DLC, EBM, ICRL, M, NcD, OSi.

c) C. P. Farrell, New York, 1892, 252p. [Also contains
"Grant Banquet," "Rev. A. Clark," and "Tribute to
Ebon C. Ingersoll."]
MiU, NN.

*d) Banner of Light, Boston, [c1899].

*e) Peter Eckler, New York, 1899.

296 THE GODS AND OTHER LECTURES.

a) C. P. Farrell, Peoria, Illinois, 1874, 253p. [First
Collected Edition. Contains "The Gods," "Humboldt,"
"Thomas Paine," "Individuality," "Heretics and
Heresies."]
CtY, DLC, FMU, ICN, IEN, IU, KU, KyWAT, MH,
MiD, MiU, NN, NjP, OCo, OO, OT, PSt, ViU.

b) George Laurie, Peoria, Illinois 1876, 253p. [Same as a)
above except for title page.]
IU, KU, OCl, OClW.

c)D. M. Bennett, New York, 1876. [Lectures
separately paged.]
DLC, MB, NN.

d) C. P. Farrell, Washington, D. C., 1878. [Same as above
except for title page.]
CtY, DLC, EBM, ICU, MiD, MiU, NN, OClW, OFH, OO.

e) Detroit Publishing Co., Detroit, 1878, 240p. [Also
contains "The Ghosts."]
MiD.

f) C. P. Farrell, New York, 1892, 253p.
MB, NN, OHi.

*g) Banner of Light, Boston, [c1899].

*h) Peter Eckler, New York, [c1899].

i) Willey Book Co., New York, 1938. [Various Pagings.
Contains the complete texts of THE GODS AND OTHER
LECTURES, THE GHOSTS AND OTHER
LECTURES, SOME MISTAKES OF MOSES, and
"WMWDTBS." Apparently from DE plates.]

297 GREAT SPEECHES (OF COL. ROBERT G.
INGERSOLL). Rhodes & McClure, Chicago, various
dates (1885, 1898, 1901, 1907), various pagings.
DLC, NcD, OCI, OCo, OFH, OT, OU, PPiU, PU, ViU.

298* GREAT THOUGHTS OF THE GREAT INGERSOLL.
Freethought Publishing Co., New York, 1928.

299 HERETICS AND HERESIES, MISTAKES OF MOSES,
PERSONAL DEISM DENIED. Garden City Book Exch.,
Chicago, n.d., 29p.
CtY.

300 THE HOUSE OF DEATH. R. Forder, London, 1897,
96p. [Funeral orations and addresses by RGI.]
ICN, NN.

301 THE INGERSOLL BIRTHDAY BOOK. Grace
MacDonald, Ed., Truth Seeker Co., New York, 1911, 233p.
[Preface by Eva Ingersoll Wakefield. Contains
many RGI passages.]
DLC.

302 INGERSOLL THE MAGNIFICENT by Joseph Lewis.
Freethought Press Assn., New York, 1957, 569p.
[Also contains SOME GEMS FROM INGERSOLL.]

303 INGERSOLL'S GREATEST LECTURES.

a) Freethought Press Assn., New York, 1944, non-consecutive paging. [Apparently from DE plates.]
b) Wehman Bros. Publishers, Hackensack, N. J., 1964, non-consecutive paging. [Apparently from DE plates.]
IEN, MB, MsU, NNC, NcD, NcU, OCl, ViU.

304 INGERSOLLIA: GEMS OF THOUGHT.

a) Belford, Clarke & Co., Chicago, 1882, 329p.
CU, CtY, FMU, ICJ, ICRL, ICU, NN.
b) G. E. Wilson, Chicago, 1892, 329p.
DLC, OC.
c) Donohue, Henneberry & Co., Chicago, 1899, 322p.
MB, MH, ViU.
d) M. A. Donohue, Chicago, [1905?], 322p.
ViU.

305 LECTURES AND ESSAYS. Watts & Co., London, 1918, 3 vols. in one, each 160p., 480p. total. [Also issued separately before 1918.]
EBM, LU, MiD, NN.

306 LECTURES OF COL. ROBERT G. INGERSOLL COMPLETE.

a) Rhodes & McClure Co., Chicago, 1896, 426p.
CU, ICRL, OCl, OO.
b) Rhodes & McClure, Chicago, 1897, 466p. [Pages numbered 429-875.] LECTURES OF COL. ROBERT G. INGERSOLL-LATEST.

307* LECTURES, SPEECHES, ESSAYS AND DEBATES.
Ram Gopal, Ed. Pioneer Press, London, [c1933].

308 LETTERS OF ROBERT G. INGERSOLL,
Eva Ingersoll Wakefield, Ed.
a) Philosophical Library, New York, 1951, 747p.
CoU, DLC, KyLE, MB, MiU, NIC, NN, NcU,
OCl, OFH, TU, TxU, ViU.
b) Watts & Co., London, 1952, 309p. [Royston Pike, Ed.]
LIFE AND LETTERS OF ROBERT G. INGERSOLL.
DLC, EBM, PP.

309 THE LIBERTY OF MAN AND OTHER ESSAYS.
Watts & Co., London, 1941, 114p.
["Thinker's Library #86."]
DLC, EBM.

310 PATRIOTIC ADDRESSES.

a) C. P. Farrell, New York, 1895, 80p.
IHi, OClWHi, OCU.
*b) Peter Eckler, New York, [c1899].

311 THE PHILOSOPHY OF INGERSOLL, Vere
Goldthwaite, Arranger. P. Elder & Co., San Francisco,
1906, 117p.
DLC, KU, MB, NN, NcD, OCl, OClW, OrU, ViU.

312 POLITICAL SPEECHES. C. P. Farrell, New York,
[1900], 582p. [Reissue of vol. 4 of DE.]
ICU, MH, NN, NNC.

313 POPULAR EDITION OF COL. INGERSOLL'S
LECTURES.

a) Freethought Publishing Co., London, 1883, 96p.
[Contains "Take a Road of Your Own," "Divine
Vivisection or Hell," "The Christian Religion," "The

Ghosts" (2 pts.), "The Apotheosis of Thomas Paine."]
EBM.
b) R. Forder, London, 1896, 80p. ["First Series." Contains
same as above except that the Thomas Paine lecture is
called "Thomas Paine the Republican."]
c) R. Forder, London, n.d. ["2nd Series." Contains "Is
All the Bible Inspired?" (2 pts.), "Mistakes of Moses,"
"Saviors of the World," "How Man Makes Gods,"
and "Law, Not God."]
d) R. Forder, London, n.d. ["3rd Series." Contains "What
Must I Do to be Saved?" (2 pts.), "The Spirit of the
Age," "Human Liberty or Intellectual Development" (2
pts.) and "Which Way?"]

314 PROSE-POEMS AND SELECTIONS FROM THE
WRITINGS AND SAYINGS OF ROBERT G.
INGERSOLL.

a) C. P. Farrell, Washington, D. C., 1884, 247p.
DLC, EBM, OC.
b) C. P. Farrell, New York, 1888, 317p. [Later eds.
have 424p.]
DLC, MB, NN, OC, OClWHi, OT, PLF, TxU.
*c) Banner of Light, Boston, [c1899].
*d) Peter Eckler, New York, [c1899].
e) Freethought Publishing Co., London,
[188-]. PROSE POEMS.

315 SELECTED SPEECHES. Regan Publishing Co.,
Chicago, 1920, 192p.
OBlC.

316 SELECTIONS FROM INGERSOLL. Ram Gopal, Ed.
G. R. Josyer, Mysore, India, 1931, 982p.
NjP.

317 SIX LECTURES BY COL. ROBERT G. INGERSOLL

  a) Abel Heywood & Son, Manchester, Eng., n.d., ["Part
  1." Contains "Mistakes of Moses," "The Ghosts,"
  "Hereafter," "Hell," "WMWDTBS," and
  "Heretics and Heresies."]
  b) Abel Heywood & Son, Manchester, Eng., n.d. ["Part
  2." Contains "Reply to Talmage," "Skulls," "Gods"
  (2 pts.), "Personal Deism Denied," and
  "Intellectual Development."]

318 SIXTY-FIVE PRESS INTERVIEWS WITH ROBERT
  G. INGERSOLL. Haldeman-Julius, Girard, Kansas,
  n.d., 150p. [Text from DE.]
  KU.

319* SPEECHES. Whitman Publishing Co.,
  Racine, Wisconsin, 1919.

320 THREE INTERESTING LECTURES: "Gods Past
  & Present," "How Gods Grow," and "The Chinese God."
  Crucible Publishing Co., Seattle, Washington,
  [c1919], 32p.

321 TOWARD HUMANITY, Anne Montgomery Traubel,
  Ed. T. B. Mosher, Portland, Maine, 1908, 86 p. [Selections
  from RGI.]
  [DLC], MH, MoKU, NN, NcD, PU.

322 WHAT IS RELIGION AND OTHER ESSAYS. Truth
  Seeker Co., New York, [190-], various pagings.
  [Contains 8 essays, all reprints of Truth Seeker
  Co. Tracts by RGI.]

323 WISDOM OF INGERSOLL.

  a) Alva A. Tanner, Ed., n.p., Oakley, Idaho, 1922, 24p.

b) Appeal to Reason, Girard, Kansas, [c1920],
61p. [People's Pocket Series #56.]
OFH.

324 WIT, WISDOM, ELOQUENCE AND GREAT
SPEECHES OF COL. ROBERT G. INGERSOLL. Rhodes
& McClure, Chicago, 1881, 67p. [Later eds. have 256 &
336p.]
DLC, ICN, IEN, IU, IaU, KU, MWA, NN,
OCl, OU, ViU.

325 WRITINGS OF ROBERT G. INGERSOLL. C. P. Farrell,
New York, 1896, various pagings [1931p. total.
Contains "The Gods and Other Lectures," "Some Mistakes
of Moses," "WMWDTBS," "Interviews on Talmage,"
"Crimes Against Criminals," and "Blasphemy."
Same material issued as parts of volumes 1-4 of DE. No
companion volumes were issued for this "vol. I."]
NN, OU.

V. Translations of Works by Ingersoll

326* *A Velt fun sotsialistisher ordnung.* Warsaw: [n.p.?], n.d., 34p. [Yiddish translation of "How to Reform Mankind."]
DLC

327* *A Welt ohne Theren.* n.place: n.p., n.d., [A Yiddish translation probably of "A World Without Tears." The content of this is unidentified.]
[OCl]

328 *Apie dieva, velnia, dangu ir pragara.* Boston: Keleivid, 1915, 26p. [Lithuanian translation of "About God, the Devil, Heaven and Hell," probably "Why I Am an Agnostic."]
[OCl]

329 *Das Weib und ihre Stellung zur Religion und Kirche am Ende des neunzehnten Jahrhunderts.* Leipzig (Germany): Schaumburg-Fleischer, 1892, 259p. [German translation of Helen Gardner's "Men, Women and Gods," with an introduction by RGI.]
NN

330 *De geesten,* Vineta, tr. Haarlem [Netherlands]: P. C. Wezel, 1894, 26p. [Dutch translation of "Ghosts."]
NN

331 *De goden*, Vineta, tr. Haarlem: P. C. Wezel, 1894, 34p.
[Dutch translation of "The Gods."]
NN

332 *Di toes'n fun Moyshe rabeynu.* [Yiddish translation
of "The Mistakes of Moses."]
*a) London: n.p., 1898, in parts.
DLC
b) London: n.p., 1910, 94p.
DLC

333 *Die Gotter*, Alois Zotz, tr. Peoria, Ill.: R. Eichenberger,
1872, 27p. [German translation of "The Gods." Issued the
same year as the lecture was first given.]
DLC

334 *Die Irrtümer Moses.* Leipzig: Schaumburg-Fleischer,
[1892], 194p. [German translation of "The
Mistakes of Moses."]

335 *Fria tankar. Föredrag o. af handler.* E. Fredin, tr.
Med biogr. inledn. Stockholm: Loonström & K.,
1884, 197p. [Swedish translation of a collection of RGI
lectures.]

336 *Fria tankar. Ny följd.* Stockholm: Loonström & K., 1885,
268p. [Swedish translation of a collection of RGI lectures.]

337* *Frie Tanker. Udvalgte populaere Föredrag.*
n.place [Denmark]: [n.p.?], 1886. [Danish translation
of a collection of RGI's lectures.]

338 *Fri Tanker for Mand, Kvinde og Born.* and
Moses Fejltageler. n.place [Denmark]: Adams Kontor,

1886. A. Moller, tr. [Danish translation of "Liberty of Man, Woman and Child" and "Mistakes of Moses."]

339 *Helvetet och spöken.* Volontaire, tr. Stockholm: Svea, 1879.
46p. [Swedish translation of "Hell" and "Ghosts."]

340 *Inch e Gronu?* Liumen, tr. Boston: n.p., 1910.
[Armenian translation of "What is Religion?"]
NN

341 *Kjaettere og Kjoetteri.* Minneapolis: C. Rasmussen, [18—], 20p. [Norwegian translation of "Heretics and Heresies."]
ICU

342 *Kyrkornas salighetsväg o. förnuftets salighetsväg.* Stockholm: Svea., 1880, 37p. [Swedish translation of "The Church's Way of Salvation and Reason's Way," probably "WMWDTBS."]

343* *Mao urinn og vélin. Islanzkao vestan hafs. Alpyo flok kurinn guf út.* Reykjavík [Iceland]: Gutenberg, 1919, 14p. [Icelandic translation of "The Man and the Machine," probably "Lay Sermon on the Labor Question."]
MH

344 *Mitä meidän pitää takeman tullaksemme pelastetuiksi.* Fitchburg, Mass.: Pohjan Tähden, 1903, 51p. [Finnish translation of "WMWDTBS."]

345* *Moderne Götterdammerung.* Leipzig: Schaumburg-Fleischer, 1891, 146p. [German translation of "The Twilight of the Gods," probably "Orthodoxy."]

346 *Mythus a Zazrak.* Prelozil Jan Razil, Nakladatelsvi Volne
Myslensky, 1929, 16p. [Czech translation of
"Myth and Miracle."]
IHi

347* *Nider mit di Farbrekher.* Vilnow, U. S. S. R.:
n.p., 1906, 30p. [Yiddish translation of "Down with the
Outlaws," probably "Crimes against Criminals."]
DLC

348 *Offener Brief an die Indianapoliser Geistlichkeit.*
Clemens Vonnegut, Sr., tr. Milwaukee: Freidenker
Publishing Co., [189-], 17p. [German translation of
"To the Indianapolis Clergy."]
NN

349* *Taenk Selv! Nogle fa punkter af det Gamle og det Ny
Testamente Kort Belyste*, Bjornstjerne Bjornson, tr.
Kristiania [Norway]: Trykt i Centraltrykk eriet, 1883, 62p.
[Norwegian translation of "Think for Yourself! A Few
Points on the Old and New Testament Briefly Explained"
probably "Foundations of Faith."]
MoKU

350 *Theologischer Nonsensometer. Ein Fragekasten fur
erwachsene Kinder u. solche, die es nicht bleiben wollen,*
Schaumburg, tr. Leipzig: Schaumburg-Fleischer, 1894, 45p.
[German translation of "Talmagian Catechism."]

351 *Valitut Teokset.* Tampereela [Finland]: M. V. Vuolukan
Kustannuksella, 1906, 330p. [Finnish
translation of ten RGI lectures.]

352* *Voltaire. Redevoering.* Amsterdam: De Dageraad, 1893,
20p. [Dutch translation of "Oration on Voltaire."]
NN

353* *Vrijheid, eene preek.* Amsterdam: De Dageraad,
1892, 23p. [Dutch translation of "Freedom, a Lecture,"
probably part of "LMWC."]
IHi, NN

354 *Was sollen wir thun um Selig zu Werden?*
Leipzig: Schaumburg-Fleischer, [c1890], 45p. [German
translation of "WMWDTBS."]
NN

VI. Works About Ingersoll

A. Biographies

Arranged Alphabetically by Author.

355 Baker, Isaac Newton. *An Intimate View of Col. Robert G. Ingersoll.* New York: C. P. Farrell, 1920, 207p. DLC, NBuU, OrU, TxLT.

356 Brown, Clarence S. *Ingersoll the Man.*
  *a) New York: C. P. Farrell, [c1903].
  b) [New York: Truth Seeker], n.d., 13p.

357 Cohen, Chapman. *Bradlaugh and Ingersoll, A Centenary Appreciation of Two Great Reformers.* London: Pioneer Press, 1933, 206p. EBM, MH, NN.

358 Cramer, Clarence H. *Royal Bob.*
  a) Indianapolis: Bobbs-Merrill, 1952, 314p. O, OC, OCl, OT, OU.
  *b) Toronto: McClelland, [c1952].

359 Gorham, Charles T. *Robert G. Ingersoll.*
  a) London: Watts & Co., 1921, 119p. EBM, IaU.
  *b) New York: Truth Seeker Co., 1928.
  *c) New York: Frederic Warne, [c1935].

d) Girard, Kansas: Haldeman-Julius, 1947, 52p. *The Life-Story of Robert G. Ingersoll.* [Abridged.]

360 Hubbard, Elbert. *Robert G. Ingersoll.* East Aurora, N. Y.: Roycrofters, 1902, 59p. [Reprinted in 1903, 1916, 1928, 1930 and possibly more often, as *Little Journey to the Home of Robert G. Ingersoll.* Also found in the "Little Journeys" series, vol. 7 *Famous Orators,* pages 231-273.]
OU.

361 Kittredge, Herman E. *Ingersoll, A Biographical Appreciation.*

a) New York: Dresden Publishing Co. [i.e. C. P. Farrell], 1911, 581p. [Issued in two bindings, one matching the DE. Included as vol. 13 of the DE after 1911.]
EBM, O, OCl, OCo.
b) Chicago: Open Court Publishing Co., 1912, 581p.
*c) Watts & Co., London, 1912.

362 Larson, Orvin. *American Infidel: Robert G. Ingersoll.* New York: Citadel Press, 1962, 316p.
O, OC, OCl, OCo, OD, OT, OU.

363 McCabe, Joseph. *Robert G. Ingersoll: Benevolent Agnostic.* Girard, Kansas: Haldeman-Julius, 1927, 64p. ["Little Blue Book #1215." From an almost simultaneous appearance in *The Haldeman-Julius Quarterly* 2:153-166 (Oct.-Dec. 1927).]

364 Macdonald, Eugene M. *Col. Robert G. Ingersoll as He Is.* New York: Truth Seeker Co., 1893, 199p. [The original appeared as a series in the *Truth Seeker* (1893).

Reissued after Ingersoll's death as *Col. Robert G. Ingersoll as He Was*, 1899.]
DLC, MH, MiU, NN.

365 Rogers, Cameron. *Colonel Bob Ingersoll*. Garden City, N. J.: Doubleday, Page & Co., 1927, 293p.
EBM, O, OC, OCl, OCo, OD, OT.

366 Sessions, Alanson. *Robert G. Ingersoll, Orator and Philosopher.*

a) Seattle: Crucible Publishing Co., 1919, 13p. [Original appearance was in *The Agnostic* 1(1), Jan. 1919.]
NN.
*b) Seattle: Raymer's, 1919, 13p.

367 Smith, Edward Garstin. *The Life and Reminiscences of Robert G. Ingersoll.*

a) New York: National Weekly Publishing Co., 1904, 225p. plus 117p. [Paged and titled separately but probably not issued as separate volumes.]
DLC, EBM, MB, OCl, TxU.
*b) New York: Peter Eckler, 1906.

368 Standring, G. *Biography of Col. Robert G. Ingersoll with Twenty Extracts from his Orations*. London: Paine Press, 1881, 12p.

369* Wheeler, Joseph Mazzini. *Life of Ingersoll* [?].
[London?]: [n.p.], 1890. [Possibly a non-existent pamphlet. See #43d.]

B. Periodical Articles

Arranged Alphabetically by Author.

370 Abbott, Lyman. "Flaws in Ingersollism." *NAR* 150:446-457 (1890).

371 Adler, Felix. "The Influence of the Late Robert G. Ingersoll." *Ethical Record* (New York) 1:26-31 (1899).

372 Angel, Donald E. "Ingersoll's Political Transition—Patriotism or Partisanship?" *Illinois State Historical Society Journal* 59:354-383 (1966).

373 Angle, P. M. "Found: The State House Corner Stone," *Illinois State Historical Society Journal* 30:260-264 (1937). [Disposes of an Ingersoll Myth.]

374 ———. "The Cornerstone Mystery Solved," *Illinois State Historical Society Journal* 37:271-283 (1944).

375 Anon. "Colonel Ingersoll and his Home." *Truth Seeker* 9:153 (1882). [From the San Francisco *Argonaut*.]

376 Anon. "Colonel Ingersoll in a Pulpit." *Truth Seeker* 23:262-263 (1896). ["On How to Reform Mankind."]

377 Anon. "Death of Robert G. Ingersoll." *Literary Digest* 19:127 (1899).

378. Anon. "Death of Robert G. Ingersoll." *Public Opinion* (Washington) 27:106 (1899).

379 Anon. "The Field-Ingersoll-Gladstone Controversy." *Public Opinion* 5:317-319 (1888).

380 Anon. "The Great Ingersoll." *Truth Seeker* 11:166-167 (1884).

381 Anon. "History as It Is Made." *Chautauquan* 29:602 (1899). [Part on RGI.]

382 Anon. "Ingersoll after Twenty Years." *Current Opinion* 71:336-338 (1921).

383 Anon. "Ingersoll and Sam Jones." *Truth Seeker* 22:262-264 (1895). [From the St. Louis *Globe Democrat*.]

384 Anon. "Ingersoll and the Religious Press." *Literary Digest* 19:197-199 (1899).

385 Anon. "Ingersoll Goes to Church." *Truth Seeker* 26:86 (1899).

386 Anon. "Ingersoll's Brain." *Truth Seeker* 7:411 (1880). [A phrenological study. From the Cincinnati *Daily Inquirer*.]

387 Anon. "Ingersoll Still Troubling the World." *Current Literature* 51:649-651 (1911).

388 Anon. "Men, Women and Events." *Cosmopolitan* 27:565-567 (1899).

389 Anon. "The Old Skepticism." *Nation* 93:313-315 (1911).

390 Anon. "A Philosophical Giant and a Theological Pigmy." *Iconoclast* (Indianapolis), n.s.? 1(1):3 (March 1882).

391 Anon. "Robert G. Ingersoll." *Irrigation Age* (Chicago) 13:373 (1899).

84

392 Anon. "Robert G. Ingersoll." *Literary Digest* 19:167-168 (1899).

393 Anon. "Robert G. Ingersoll." *Outlook* 62:696-698 (1899).

394 Anon. "The Spurgeon of Negation." *Spectator* 83:148-149 (1899).

395 Anon. "A Study of Colonel Ingersoll." *Review of Reviews* 20:355 (1899).

396 Austin, F. "Colonel Robert G. Ingersoll." *Sermon* 4:617-624 (1903).

397 Beach, Stuart. "Apostles of Liberty." *Independent* 118:640 (1927).

398 Bergengren, Ralph. "Robert G. Ingersoll." *National Magazine* (Boston) 10:606-608 (1899).

399 Boucher, W. M. "Facts and Truths." *Open Court* 3:1620-1622 (1889).

400 Bradlaugh, Charles. "Mr. Gladstone's Reply to Colonel Ingersoll On Christianity." *Our Corner* (London) 12:1-8 (1888). [This seems to be the only article ever written by England's greatest freethinker about America's greatest freethinker. Ingersoll seems to never have published anything on Bradlaugh (1833-1891).]

401 Brann, Henry. "Robert G. Ingersoll." *Catholic World* 69:787-790 (1899).

402 [Brooks, Van Wyck.] "A Reviewer's Note-book." *Freeman* 2:311 (1921).

85

403 Chapman, Edward M. "Robert G. Ingersoll, Theologian."
Forum 48:339-353 (1912).

404 Cobern, Rev. Camden M. "Mr. Ingersoll's Use of the
Bible." *Homiletic Review* 38:491-497 (1899).

405 Colonus [pseud.] "Ingersoll's Philosophy." *Light*
(London) 11:82-83 (1891).

406 Cook, Col. V. Y. "Forrest's Capture of Col. R. G.
Ingersoll." *Confederate Veteran* 15:54-55 (1907).

407 Cramer, C. H. "Robert Green Ingersoll." *Papers in Illinois
History* (1940):58-68.

408 ———. "The Political Metamorphosis of Robert G.
Ingersoll." *Illinois State Historical Society Journal*
36:271-283 (1943).

409 Crocker Lionel. "Robert Green Ingersoll's Influence on
American Oratory." *Quarterly Journal of Speech*
24:299-312 (1943).

410 [Dale, Samuel S.] "Both the Goods and the Money."
Textile World Record 48:47-48 (Dec. 1914). [On RGI's
steel rails simile in his Lincoln lecture.]

411 Dashiell, T. G. "Immortality in the Old Testament." *NAR*
146:224-225 (1888).

412 Debs, Eugene V. "Robert G. Ingersoll." *American Journal
of Politics* 2:198-202 (1893).

413 ———. "Recollections of Ingersoll." *Pearson's Magazine*
(London), April 1917, 302-307.

414 Dibble, R. F. "The Devil's Advocate." *American Mercury* 3:64-70 (Sept. 1924).

415 Farrar, Frederic William. "A Few Words on Colonel Ingersoll." *NAR* 150:594-608 (1890).

416 Fawcett, Edgar. "To Robert G. Ingersoll." *The Arena* 9:114-117 (1893). [A poem.]

417 ———. "Robert G. Ingersoll." *Truth Seeker* 21:23 (1894). [A poem. From *The Arena.*]

418 Field, Rev. Henry M. "The Influence of Ingersoll." *NAR* 112:322-328 (1899).

419 Finkel, William Leo. "Robert Ingersoll's Oratory and Walt Whitman's Poetry." *Speech Monographs* 16:41-56 (1949).

420 Forcythe, Stillman. "Col. Ingersoll and Christianity." *NAR* 146:103 (1888).

421 Gardener, Helen H. "Robert Ingersoll the Builder." *Freethought* (San Francisco) 2:137-138 (1889).

422 [Gillis, J. M.] " 'Bob' Ingersoll." *Catholic World* 121:216-226 (1925).

423 Godwin, George. "Ingersoll: The Great Agnostic." *American Rationalist* 4:11-13 (1959).

424 Graeff, I. E. "Historic Glances at Ingersollism." *Reformed Church Quarterly Review* 27:602-623 (1880).

425 Hall, A. Oakey. "The 'Cui Bono' of Infidelity." *Catholic World* 66:505-509 (1897).

426 Hatton, Joseph. "An Englishman's View of Ingersoll." *Truth Seeker* 10:6-7 (1883).

427 Hawthorne, Rev. J. B. "An Answer to Ingersoll" *Homiletic Review* 35:418-423 (1898).

428* Herndon, E. W. "Robert G. Ingersoll in the *North American Review.*" *Christian Quarterly* (Mo.) 1:72- (1882).

429 Hughes, James L. "World Leaders I Have Known." *Canadian Magazine* 60:563-570 (1923).

430 Kaye, Rev. J. R. "Ingersoll's Philosophy of the Bible—An Examination of the Lecture 'About the Holy Bible.' " *Freethought Magazine* (Chicago), In several parts: 13:309-322, 377-389, 432-441, 502-509, 555-559, 624-629, 683-690. (1895), 14:29-37 (1896).

431 Kittredge, Herman E. "Ingersoll—An Appreciation." *Truth Seeker* 26:6-7 (1899). [From the St. Louis *Medical Brief.*]

432 ———. "Ingersoll: His Genius, Philosophy, Humanity and Influence." *The Arena* 31:50-69 (1904).

433 ———. "Ingersoll as an Idealist." *The Arena* 31:244-261 (1904).

434 [LaMaster, W. H.] "Ingersollism." *Iconoclast* [n.s.?] 1(1):4 (March 1882).

435 LeSueur, W. D. "Foot-Prints of Creative Power." *NAR* 146:219 (1888).

436 Macdonald, E. M. "Ingersoll and his Traducers." *Truth Seeker* 23:39-40 (1896). [Later continued as "Ingersoll as He Is."]

437 ———. "Ingersoll as He Is." *Truth Seeker* 23:54-55, 70-72, 86-88, 102-104, 118-121 (1896).

438 Marshall, C. A. "Open Letter to Col. Robert G. Ingersoll on the Financial Question." *Truth Seeker* 7:411 (1880).

439 Martin, E. S. "This Busy World." *Harper's Weekly* 43:758, 761 (1899). [Part on RGI.]

440 Monahan, Michael. "*In Re* Colonel Ingersoll." *Papyrus* Somerville, N.J.) 4(2):1-17 (1905).

441 Myall, William. "Mr. Ingersoll as a Reformer." *International Review* 12:225-240 (1882).

442 Nolan, Paul T. "A Southerner's Tribute to Illinois' 'Pagan Prophet.'" *Illinois State Historical Society Journal* 51:268-283 (1958).

443 North, J. W. "Robert G. Ingersoll and his Critics." *Freethought* 2:311-313, 325-327 (1889).

444 O'Connor, Richard. "Bob Ingersoll, The Devil's Ambassador." *American Mercury* 69:586-593 (1949).

445 Peck, Harry Thurston. "Robert G. Ingersoll." *Bookman* 10:24-30 (1899).

446 ———. "A Remarkable Estimate of Ingersoll." *Ave Maria* (South Bend, Ind.), n.s. 49:403-406 (1899).

447 Rankin, J. E. "Satan's Morning Greeting." *Our Day* 3:473-475 (1889). [A poem.]

448 Ricker, Marilla M. "Robert G. Ingersoll." *The Fra*
3:67-70 (1909).

449 Savage, Minot J. "Mr. Savage on Ingersoll." *Free Thought
Magazine* 14:20-25 (1896). [From the Boston *Post.*]

450 Schilling, G. A. "Ingersoll and the Anarchists—Important
Testimony." *Lucifer Magazine* (Chicago) Series 3,
7:139 (1903).

451 Schinz, A. "Un Champion De L'Incredulité Aux Etats—
Unis D' Amerique." *Revue de Théologie et de Philosophie*
(Geneva) 32:512-535 (1899).

452 Schroeder, Theodore. "Robert Ingersoll's Conservatism."
Freeman 2:498 (1921).

453 Sessions, Alanson. "In Defence of Robert Ingersoll."
Freeman 2:402 (1921).

454 Simonds, Rev. W. D. "Ingersoll's Power with the People."
Non-Sectarian 3:256-260 (1893).

455 Spalding, Bishop J. L. "God in the Constitution—A Reply
to Col. Ingersoll." *The Arena* 1:517-528 (1890).

456 Strickler, W. C. "Colonel Ingersoll and Dr. Slade." *Light*
19:456 (1899).

457 Sunderland, Rev. J. T. "Robert Ingersoll After Nine Years:
A Study." *The Arena* 41:295-301 (1909).

458 Swancara, Frank. "The Work of Ingersoll." *Truth Seeker*
39:33-34 (Jan. 20, 1912).

459 [Taussig, F. W.] "The Lincoln Tariff Myth Finally Disposed Of." *Quarterly Journal of Economics* 35:500 (1921).

460 Townsend, Rev. C. W. "Ingersoll Versus Paul." *Homiletic Review* 37:134-137 (1899).

461 Underwood, B. F. "Ingersoll." *The Index* (Boston), n.s., 4:568-569 (1884).

462 Various Authors. "The Combat for the Faith: The Field-Ingersoll-Gladstone Controversy." *NAR* 147:1-36 (1888). [Five articles by different authors.]

463 Vater, Thomas G. "Ingersoll vs. Christianity." *Universalist Quarterly* 40:291-303 (1883).

464 Ward, Rev. William Hayes. "Colonel Ingersoll." *Review of Reviews* 20:317-320 (1899).

465 Watts, Charles "Realistic Freethought in America— Colonel Robert G. Ingersoll." *Secular Review* (London) 14:18-19 (1884). [Also printed in the *Truth Seeker* 11:67 (1884).]

466 Wettstein, Otto. "The Beneficence of Ingersoll." *Truth Seeker* 23:230-231 (1894).

467 Zerbe, L. R. "Colonel Ingersoll on Christianity." *NAR* 146:344 (1888).

C. Non-Biographical Books and Pamphlets

Arranged Alphabetically by Author.

468 *Anon. (A spiritualist). *Jesus and Ingersoll.* [n. place: n.p., 1880?].

469 Anon. *Ingersoll Memorial Souvenir: Programme, Grand Opera House, Chicago* (*Oct. 20,* [1901], *2:30 P.M.*), Chicago: Geo. K. Hazlitt & Co., 1901, 16p.

470 Anon. *Christ Versus Ingersoll.* St. Paul, Minn.: Twin Cities Secularists, [c1960], 2p. [Leaflet.]

471 Applebee, James Kay. *Col. Robert G. Ingersoll and His Chicago Critics: A Lecture . . . . Delivered May 4,1879.* Chicago: A. B. Case & Sons, [c1879]. OCHi.

472 Banes, Warren C. *The Death-Bed Conversion of Robert G. Ingersoll.* Chicago: American Secular Union [c1910], 16p. NN.

473 Benlisa, Samuel. *I Am That I Am, or Mr. Ingersoll vs. The Jehovah of the Jews.* Jacksonville, Florida: Union Job Rooms, 1884, 39p. DLC.

474 Berkowitz, Henry. *Judaism and Ingersollism.* Philadelphia: n.p., 1894, 6p. NN.

475 Bertron, Mrs. Ottille. *Review of Colonel Robert G. Ingersoll's Attacks Upon Christianity.* Philadelphia: Author, 1889, 112p. DLC.

476 Bethune, James N. *Mistakes of Ingersoll.* New York: Author, 1882, 150p. DLC.

477 Bien, Herman Milton, *Lying Made Easy: A Reply to Ingersoll's "Mistakes of Moses" and "Skulls," being a defence of the Bible . . . . A Lecture . . . Delivered April 27, 1879.* Chicago: A.B. Case & Son, 1879, 15p. OCH.

478 Bierce, Ambrose. ("A Dead Lion"), *The Collected Works of Ambrose Bierce.* vol. 10. New York & Washington: Neale Publishing Co., 1909-12, p. 212-233. OU.

479 Black, John W. *Col. Ingersoll's Reply to Gladstone Briefly Criticised.* London: F. Verinder, 1889, 16p. EBM.

480 Bland, Thomas Augustus. ("Robert G. Ingersoll,") *Pioneers of Progress.* Chicago: Author, 1906, 254p. OCl.

481 Braden, Clark. *Ingersoll Unmasked: A Scathing and Fearless Expose of His Life and Real Character.*

a) New York: Author, 1886, 16p. NN, OCHi.
b) Lexington, Ky.: Blue Grass Printing Co., 1900, 129p. DLC.

482 ———. *Christianity Defended: A Lecture by Prof. Clark Braden, Reviewing Col. Ingersoll's Lecture on "The Gods."* Peoria, Illinois: n.p., n.d., 25p.

483 Bradlaugh, William R. *The Mistakes of Ingersoll: Genesis.* London: J. Snow & Co.: W. R. Bradlaugh, [1897], 27p. EBM.

484 Brann, Rev. Henry A. *The Age of Unreason: Being a Reply to Thomas Paine, Robert G. Ingersoll, Felix Adler, Rev. O. B. Frothingham and other American Rationalists.* New York: M. B. Brown, 1881, [2nd ed. Unable to locate a copy of 1st ed.] NN.

485 Brann, William Cowper. *Brann the Iconoclast.* Waco, Texas: C. C. Womack & Co., 1899, 2 vols. [On RGI: "Apostle vs. Pagan," vol. 1: 34-37, "Prayers for the Pagan," vol. 2: 462-464]. OCl, OCo, OT, OU.

486 Briggs, G. W. *Ingersoll and Ingersollism: A Lecture Delivered in the Tremont Opera House, Galveston Texas, May 13, 1880.* Galveston: Clarke & Courts, 1880, 12p. DLC, NN.

487 Brown, Charles O. *Brown vs. Ingersoll, Did the Great Infidel Petition for Repeal of the Laws against Obscenity?* Dubuque, Iowa: [*Dubuque Daily Times*], [c1888], 8p. NN.

488 Bryan, Rev. Edward. *Ingersoll on Orthodoxy: A Reply.* Bradford, Pa.: W. F. Jordan, 1884, 55p. DLC.

489 Buchanan, John. *Ingersoll's Moses' Mistakes Criticised.* Aukland, New Zealand: J. H. Field, [188-?], 39p. NN.

490 Buckley, J. M. *Ingersoll Under the Microscope.*

　a) Cincinnati: Cranston & Curts, 1892, 36p. DLC, OO.
*b) New York: Methodist Book Co., [c1902].

491 Caldwell, Rev. J. H. *Ingersollism Brought Face to Face with Christianity.* Willmington, Del.: James Webb Printing & Stationery Co., 1881, 47p. DLC.

492 Carr, C. E. *My Day and Generation*. Chicago: McClurg, 1908, 452p. [RGI on pages 310-312, 331-338.]

493 Carson, Rev. J. F. *Ingersoll and the Bible*. Brooklyn, N. Y.: S. H. Berry, 1895, 23p. [2nd ed. Unable to locate copy of 1st Ed.] NN.

494 Cochran, P. A. *A Critical Criticiser Criticised; or Ingersoll's Gospel Analysed*. St. Albans, Vt.: [n.p.], 1900, 127p. [Contains RGI's "WMWDTBS."] NCo, NN.

495 Colcord, Samuel. *Reply to Ingersoll*. New York: W. Hauptmann, [1899], 32p. DLC.

496 Coleman, William M. *The Gospel According to Ingersoll*. Washington: n.p., 1881, 8p. DLC.

497 Conway, Moncure D. *My Pilgrimage to the Wise Men of the East*. Boston: Houghton, Mifflin & Co., 1906, [Page 15-24 on Ingersoll.] OU.

498 Crafts, Wilbur Fisk & Chaplain McCabe. *Ten Points of Ingersollville*. Chicago: Rhodes and McClure, 1879, 47p. DLC.

499 Cross, Philip. *Some Mistakes of Ingersoll; or Moses on Top*. Newark, N. J.: Advertiser Printing House, 1894, 36p. DLC, EBM, NN.

500 Curtiss, Samuel I. *Ingersoll and Moses*. Chicago: Jansen McClurg & Co., 1880, 188p. DLC, EBM, NN.

501 Dabney, Robert L. *The Latest Infidelity: A Reply to Ingersoll's Position*. Richmond, Va.: Presbyterian Committee of Publication, 1888, 68p. DLC, EBM.

502 Debs, Eugene V. *Pastels of Men.* New York: Pearson's, 1919, 63p. [Part on RGI.] NN.

503 Dement, R. S. *Ingersoll, Beecher and Dogma; or A Few Simple Truths. . . .* Chicago: S. C. Griggs & Co., 1878, 155p. DLC, EBM, MiD, NN.

504 Dietrich, John Hassler. *Robert G. Ingersoll: An Appreciation.* Minneapolis, Minn.: First Unitarian Society, 1929, 16p. [Pages numbered 81-96.] In *The Humanist Pulpit,* Series 12 #6.] NN.

505 Dixon, Thomas. *Dixon on Ingersoll.*

   a) New York: John B. Alden, 1892, 198p.
 b) Ten Sermons on Ingersoll. New York: J. S. Ogilvie, [c1902].

506 Douglas, Caroline M. *Reply to Col. Ingersoll's "What Shall I Do To Be Saved?"* London: Simpkin, Marshall & Co., [1881], 46p. EBM.

507 Dowling, M. E. *Reason and Ingersollism.* Detroit: William Graham Printers, 1882, 170p. DLC, EBM.

508 Drake, Allison. *Mr. Ingersoll and What He Vilifies.* Newport, Ky.: Author, 1892, 25p. DLC, EBM.

509 Duganne, Augustine J. H. *Injuresoul; A Satire for Science.* New York: American Bookprint Co., 1884, 214p. [A poem.] DLC, OU.

510 Dungan, D. R. *Ingersoll's Mistakes about Moses.*

   a) Cincinnati: Central Book Concern, 1879, 35p. DLC.
 b) Mistakes of Ingersoll about Moses. St. Louis: Christian Publishing Co., [c1902.]

511 Dunnett, S. *A Jaw-Breaker for Ingersoll and His Infidel Confederates*. Solomon City, Kansas: Sentinel Print, 1882, 60p. DLC.

512 Edgett, George W. *The Mistakes of Robert G. Ingersoll on Nature and God*. Boston: Beacon Press, 1881, 37p. DLC.

513 Evans, Frederick William. *Robert G. Ingersoll for 1892*. Mt. Lebanon, N. Y.: n.p., 1892, 4p. NN.

514 Finley, Merrill. *Christ and the Colonel*. Girard, Kansas: Haldeman-Julius, 1948, 120p. [Contains many extracts from RGI's works.]

515 [Fisher, Sydeny G.] *Ingersoll Answered*. Philadelphia: D. J. Gallagher, 1889, 29p. DLC.

516 Foote, George William. *Ingersollism Defended Against Archdeacon Farrar*. London: R. Forder, 1892, 16p. NN.

517 ———. *Dr. Torrey and the Infidels*. London: Pioneer Press, 1905, 16p. [Part on RGI.] NN.

518 Fulton, John D. *The Surrender to Infidelity . . . The Breathings of the Pit: A Reply to Robert G. Ingersoll*. New York: Funk & Wagnalls, 1884, 38p. [On RGI: pages 27-38.] EBM.

519 Furlong, John Ryan. *Is Ingersoll in Hell?* Boulder, Colorado: Author, 1909, 20p. [DLC has 2nd Ed., 1910, 183p.] NN.

520 Garland, Hamlin, ("Lowell, Ingersoll and Booth")
Roadside Meetings. New York: Macmillan, 1931,
pages 44-48 on RGI. OC, OCl, OD, OT, OU.

521 Gilbert, James Eleazer. *Which Way, or Ingersoll's
Argument for Christianity—Delivered Feb. 27, 1885.*
Grand Rapids, Mich.: n.p., 1885, 7p. NN.

522 Gladstone, William E. ("Ingersoll on Christianity")
Later Gleanings. New York: Charles Scribner's Sons,
1897, 426p. [Pages 118-158 on RGI.]

523 Goodwin, Edward Payson. *Christianity and Infidelity
Tested by Their Fruits.* Chicago: Advance Publishing Co.,
1880, 35p. NN.

524 Griffith, William, Ed. *Idols of Egypt.* Carbondale, Illinois:
Egypt Book House, 1947, 201p. ["The Great Agnostic"
by B. B. Hubbs.] NN.

525 Gripenberg, Baroness Alexandra (of Finland). *A Half
Year in the New World.* Newark, Del.: University
of Delaware Press, 1954, 225p. [Pages 91-95 on RGI.]

526* Guiteau, Charles J. *A Reply to Ingersoll's Attack on the
Bible.* Philadelphia: [n.p.?], 1878.

527 Guss, Rev. John. *Common-Place Strictures on Col.
Ingersoll's Lecture on "Intellectual Development."*
Harrisburg, Pa.: Central Pennsylvania M. E. Book Room,
1878, 24p. DLC.

528 Hall, John G. *Shakespeare Versus Ingersoll.* Cleveland:
The Burrow Bros. Co., 1888, 43p. [EBM], NN.

529 Hannon, James C. *An Appreciation and Defense of the Late Col. Robert G. Ingersoll.* Philadelphia: n.p., 1924, 23p.

530 Hastings, H. L. *Remarks on the "Mistakes of Moses."* [Boston]: Scriptural Tract Repository, 1882, 33p. DLC.

531 Herring, Needham Bryan. *Ingersoll and the Deist.*
a) Wilson, N. C.: D. Herring, 1889, 101p. DLC, NN.
*b) New York: Ketcham, [c1899].

532 [Holms, C. W.] *Jesus and Ingersoll in the Open Court.* New York: Truth Seeker Co., 1899, 44p. NN.

533 Hubbard, Elbert. *The Olympians: A Tribute to Tall Sun Crowned Men.* East Aurora, N. Y.: Roycrofters, [c1921], pages 49-55 on RGI. OCl.

534 Hudson, Jay William ("A Day with Ingersoll"), *Christianity, A Continuing Calamity.* Girard, Kansas: Haldeman-Julius, 1950, 31p. [Pages 16-17 on RGI.]

535 Husted, Harvey. *Robert G. Ingersoll's Religious Teachings.* White Plains, N. Y.: Author, [1925?], 62p. DLC, NN.

536 Ingersoll Monument Assn. *Unveiling the Statue of Robert G. Ingersoll at Glen Oak Park, Peoria, Illinois, Saturday, October 28, 1911.* [Peoria: n.p., 1911?], 33p.

537 Insane Johnny [Pseud. of John G. Miller]. *Mistakes of Robert G. Ingersoll.* Des Moines, Iowa: Mills & Co., 1881, 15p. DLC, NN.

538 [Izant], Grace Goulder. *Ohio Scenes and Citizens.* Cleveland: World Publishing Co., [1964], 253p. [Pages 40-51 on RGI.] OCHi.

539 Jerris, Prof. Frank I. *Ten Thousand Dollars Wanted From Col. Robert G. Ingersoll and the Reasons Why He Should Pay It.* Chicago: n.p., 1888, 110p. DLC.

540 John, John Price Durbin. *Did Man Make God or Did God Make Man, A Reply to Robert G. Ingersoll.* Indianapolis: Frank Caldwell, 1898, 100p. DLC.

541 Johnson, Prof. H. U. *What Must We Do To Be Saved? or Paul Against Ingersoll.* Jamestown, N. Y.: Chautauqua Democrat Print, 1881, 19p. DLC.

542 Jones, Edgar D. ("Robert G. Ingersoll"), *Lords of Speech.* Chicago: Willett, Clark & Co., 1937. [RGI on pages 149-162.] OU.

543 Keyser, John H. *Reason vs. Revelation from the Fulcrum of the Spirit Philosophy, A Reply to Robert G. Ingersoll.* New York: J. J. Little & Co., 1888, 146p. DLC, NN.

544 Kramer, Zebi Hirsch. *An Open Letter to Robert G. Ingersoll.* San Francisco: n.p., 1888, 8p. NN.

545 Lacy, B. W. *Reply to Rev. L. A. Lambert's "Notes on Ingersoll."* Philadelphia: Keystone Publishing Co., 1885, 184p. DLC, MiD, NN.

546 Lambert, Louis Aloisius. *Notes on Ingersoll.*

a) Buffalo, N. Y.: Buffalo Catholic Publishing Co., 1884, 200p. DLC, EBM, O, OCHi.
b) *Lambert's Reply to Ingersoll.* Huntington, Indiana: Our Sunday Visitor, [c1929], 63p. OC.
c) *Answers to Atheists.* London & New York: Burns & Oates, Ltd., [1884?], 203p.

547 ———. *Tactics of Infidels.* Buffalo: P. Paul & Brothers, 1887, 357p. NN, O.

548 ———. *Rev. L. A. Lambert, LLD Versus Col. Robert G. Ingersoll.* Cleveland: Universe Publishing Co., [c1890], 216p. [Introduction by Rt. Rev. J. L. Spalding.] NN.

549 ———. *Ingersoll's Christmas Sermons.* Akron, O.: D. H. McBride, 1898, 216p. DLC.

550 Leech, S. V., DD. *Magnificent Reply to Robert G. Ingersoll's Attack on the Bible.* New York: I. K. Funk & Co., 1879, 10p. NN.

551 Lellyett, John. *Letters to the Goliath of Gas, Better Known in Modern Times as Robert G. Ingersoll.* Nashville, Tenn.: Publishing House of M. E. Church, 1890, 155p. DLC, EBM.

552 Lewis, Joseph. *Gems from Ingersoll. Address Delivered over Radio Station WGBS.* [New York: Freethought Press Assn., 1926], 2L.

553 Lucas, Helen M. *View of Lambert's "Notes on Ingersoll."* New York: Truth Seeker Co., 1909, 237p. OCl, OHi.

554 Lydick, Ernest B. *The Souls of Ingersoll and Joan of Arc.* Pittsburgh, Pa.: Lydick, Turner & Co., 1916, 94p. [2nd ed.] [First ed. as *Where is the Soul of Ingersoll?* Copy not located.]

555 Magruder, A. B. *The Bible Defended and Atheism Rebuked. A Reply to Robert G. Ingersoll's Lectures on "Mistakes of Moses" and "What Must We Do To Be Saved?"* Chicago: C. H. Jones, 1881, 246p. DLC, EBM.

556 Mansfield, I. Delos. *A Review of Robert G. Ingersoll's Lecture on "Orthodoxy."* [California: n.p., 1884.] [A sermon Delivered at St. Paul's Church, Benicia, Calif., 1884.] CU.

557 Marble, David H. *Answer to Ingersoll.* [Boston]: n.p., [c1885], 18p. DLC.

558 Martin, Lafayette. *Ingersoll at the Barricades.* [Kankakee, Ill.]: Kankakee Gazette Book Office, [1886], 12p. DLC.

559 Marty, Martin E. ("Infidelity Incarnate: Robert Ingersoll") *The Infidel: Freethought and American Religion.* Cleveland: World Publishing Co., 1961, 224p. [Pages 137-150 on RGI.] O, OC, OCl, OCo.

560 Masters, Edgar Lee. ("Robert G. Ingersoll"), *The Great Valley.* New York: Macmillan, 1916. [A poem on p. 77.] O, OCl, OCo, OD, OT, OU.

561 McClure, J. B. Ed. *Mistakes of Ingersoll.*

a) Chicago: Rhodes & McClure, 1879, 2 vols. bound as one, 118p., & 151p. [Replies of various ministers to RGI.] DLC.
b) Chicago: Rhodes & McClure, 1882, 4 vols. bound as one, 118p., 151p., 32p. & 158p. [Last two sections are replies of ministers to "WMWDTBS" and "Thomas Paine."] DLC.
c) *Mistakes of Ingersoll on Thomas Paine.* Chicago: Rhodes & McClure, 1880, 158p. [Section 4 of b above only.] DLC.

562 —— Ed. *Ingersoll's New Departure, Replies to his Famous Lecture "What Must We Do To Be Saved?"*

Chicago: Rhodes & McClure, 1880, 92p. plus 32p.
of "WMWDTBS." DLC.

563 McGrady, Thomas. *The Mistakes of Ingersoll.*

a) Cincinnati: Curts & Jennings, 1898, 344p. DLC, EBM.
*b) New York: Methodist Book Co., [c1899].
*c) Chicago: Rhodes, [c1899].

564 Mitchell, Thomas. *Conflict of the Nineteenth Century—
The Bible and Freethought.* New York: Universal Book
Co., 1893, 456p. DLC, NN, OC.

565 Monahan, Michael. *Palms of Papyrus.* East Orange, N. J.:
Papyrus Publishing Co., 1909. [Contains "*In Re
Col. Ingersoll,*" reprinted from *The Papyrus*] [See #440].
OCl, OT, OU.

566 ———. *An Attic Dreamer.* New York: Mitchell Kennerley,
1922. [Contains same as above.] [See #440].
O, OCl, OD, OT, OU.

567 Morton, J. F. & Franklin Steiner. *The Case of Billy Sunday.*
New York: Truth Seeker Co., 1915. [RGI on pages 13-15,
22-32.]

568 Mountain Laburnium [Pseud.?] *A Woman's Battle With
Bob Ingersoll.* Cincinnati: Author, 1884, 23p. DLC.

569 Ness, Lizzie G. *Ness Versus Ingersoll: Another View
of the Suicide Question.* Hartford, Conn.: n.p., [189-?],
52p. NN.

570 Nevin, Alfred. *Letters Addressed to Col. Robert G.
Ingersoll or Infidelity Rebuked and Truth Victorious.*
Philadelphia: P. W. Ziegler & Co., 1882, 232p. DLC.

571 North, Thomas LeRoy. *Is Death a Beginning or the End?*
Greenville, Ohio: Author, [c1934], 43p. DLC.

572 Northgraves, G. R. *Mistakes of Modern Infidels.*

a) Philadelphia: J. E. Potter Co., 1885, 432p.
b) Toronto: J. S. Robertson & Brothers, 1886, 432p.
[2nd Ed.] EBM.

573 Oliver, Robert. ("Robert G. Ingersoll"), *A History of
Public Speaking in America.* Boston: Allyn & Bacon, 1965.
[Pages 342-349 on RGI. O, OC, OCl, OU.

574 Owen, Rev. Olin Marvin. *Ingersoll Answered from the
Bible and Ingersoll Against Himself.* Saratoga Springs,
N. Y.: John Johnson & Co., 1886, 228p. DLC, OCl.

575 Parker, Joseph, DD. *Ingersoll Answered. . . .* London:
C. B. Hunt, 1881, 62p. EBM, NN.

576 Parrish, Wayland Maxfield & Alfred Dwight Huston.
("Robert G. Ingersoll"), *History and Criticism of
American Public Address.* W. N. Brigance, Ed. New York:
McGraw-Hill, 1943, 2 vols. [RGI in vol. I, pages
363-386.] OC, OCl, OT, OU.

577 Pearne, Rev. Thomas Hall. *God in the Constitution*:
A Review of Col. Robert G. Ingersoll. Cincinnati: n.p.,
1890, 23p. OClWHi.

578 Platt, W. H. *God Out and Man In*; *or Replies to Robert G.
Ingersoll.* Rochester, N. Y.: Steele & Avery, 1883. EBM.

579 ———. *Inspiration*: *An Imaginary Symposium Between
Col. Ingersoll and a Lawyer.* San Francisco: n.p., 1882,
19p. ["For private distribution."] DLC.

580 Potter, Charles F. *The Story of Religion as Told in the Lives of its Leaders.* Garden City, N. Y.: Garden City Publishing Co., 1929, 627 p. [RGI on pages 545-551.] OU.

581 ———. *Great Religious Leaders.* New York: Simon & Shuster, 1958. [Pages 421-425 on RGI.] O, OC, OCo, OT, OU.

582 Pringle, Alan. *Ingersoll in Canada.*

  a) Napanee, [Ontario]: Standard Book & Job Co., 1880, 56p.
  *b) New York: Truth Seeker Co., [c1884].

583 Putnam, Samuel Porter. *Ingersoll and Jesus.* New York: Truth Seeker Co., [c1885], 10p. [A poem.]

584 Rationalist, A [Pseud.] *A Refutation of Col. Robert G. Ingersoll's Lectures.* Toronto: n.p., 1880, 20p.

585 Redwine, Fletcher H. *The Infidel Boomerang Tested: or A Review of Robert G. Ingersoll's Printed Lecture "What Must We Do To Be Saved?"* n.place: [I. T. Tussy?], 1902, 58p. DLC.

586 Ricker, Marilla. *Robert G. Ingersoll.* [Chicago: The Liberal Review Co., 1906] 11p. [Original in *The Liberal Review* (Chicago) 3:204-211 (1906.] DLC.

587 ———. *The Four Gospels.*

  a) East Aurora, N. Y.: Roycrofters, 1911. [Contains 45p. section on RGI.] DLC, OU.
  b) *Paine and Ingersoll.* New York: Truth Seeker Co., 1912.

588 Roberts, John Emerson. *Ingersoll and His Times.* Kansas City, Mo.: Gerard & Brown, [190-?], 26p. NN.

589 ———. *Ingersoll and His Work For Humanity*. Chicago: Chicago Society of Rationalism, n.d., 24p.

590 ———. *What Must We Do To Be Saved?* Kansas City, Mo.: n.p., n.d., 16p.

591 Roberts, William C. ("Robert G. Ingersoll"), *Leading Orators of Twenty-five Campaigns*. New York: L. K. Strouse & Co. [Pages 248-250 on RGI.] O, OCHi, OD, OU.

592 Rothacker, Ottomar Hebern. *Some Phases, A Review of Ingersoll and His Methods*. Washington: Hatchet Publishing Co., 1886, 60p. DLC.

593 Rubi, Rev. M. *Ingersollism In Its True Colors*. Buffalo, N. Y.: Buffalo Catholic Publishing Co., 1886, 82p. DLC.

594 Rusterholtz, Wallace P. *American Heretics and Saints*. Boston: Manthorne & Burack, 1938, 362. [Pages 216-250 on RGI.] O, OCo.

595 See, Isaac M. *Zion, The Sunny Mount, Ingersoll, The Bible, Christians*. Brooklyn, N. Y.: n.p., [18 - -], 27p. NN.

596 Shaw, Warren C. ("Robert G. Ingersoll"), *History of American Oratory*. Indianapolis: Bobbs-Merrill, 1928. [Pages 443-480 on RGI.] O, OC, OCl, OCo, OD, OT, OU.

597 Sparks, S. *Sparks vs. Ingersoll*. Camden, N. J.: J. Millette, 1897, 55p. [Ed. of 1899 also contains Sparks' lecture on G. Washington, 74p.] DLC.

598 Stephens, E. *Infidelity Disarmed*. . . . Toronto: n.p., 1900, 255p. EBM, NCo.

599 Stevenson, Adlai E. *Something of Men I Have Known.* Chicago: McClurg. 1909, 442p. [Pages 225-228, 273-274, 378-380 on RGI.]

600 Stickley, W. W. *An Open Letter to Robert G. Ingersoll.* Baltimore, Md.: n.p., 1894, 9p. DLC, NN.

601 Stuart, John C. *Ingersoll's "Ghosts," An Examination of Robert G. Ingersoll's Objections to the Bible.* London: T. Woolmer, 1885, 45p. EBM.

602 Sunderland, Rev. J. T. *Robert G. Ingersoll's Treatment of "The Bible."* Ann Arbor, Mich.: J. T. Sunderland, 1895 (April). ["College Town Pulpit," Series one, Number 8.]

603 ———. *Robert Ingersoll: His Moral and Religious Influence.* Oakland, Calif.: A Pacific Coast Pulpit, Vol. 1 #6, [1899]. DLC.

604 Tiffany, Joel. *Review of Col. Ingersoll's Lecture on the Question What Shall We Do To Be Saved?* Chicago: Chicago Legal News Co., 1881, 22p.

605* Trenwith, William H. *Ethics and Atheists or Remonstrances with Professor Adler, Col. Ingersoll and Others.* New York: J. W. Pratt, 1881.

606 Waters, Richard Rawlings. *Some Mistakes of Ingersoll.* Newport, Ky.: Newport Printing Co., 1886, 24p. DLC.

607 Watchtower Bible and Tract Society. *Thy Word is Truth. An Answer to Robert Ingersoll's Charges Against Christianity.* Allegheny, Pa.: Watchtower Bible & Tract Society, 1892, 32p. NN, OO.

608 Watts, Charles. *American Freethinkers*. London: Watts & Co., [c1885], 16p. NN.

609 Wendling, G. R. *Ingersollism from a Secular Point of View*. Chicago: Jansen, McClurg & Co., 1883, 130p. DLC, EBM, NN.

610 Wharton, Henry Marvin. *Moody and Ingersoll*. Kansas City, Mo.: Tiernan-Havens Printing Co., 1900, 64p. DLC.

611 Whitaker, Robert. *The Man Who Might Have Been: A Lost Biography*. San Francisco: Whitaker & Ray Co., 1899, 21p. [First part on RGI, 2nd on David Swing.] DLC.

612 Whitman, C. M. ("Robert G. Ingersoll"), *American Orators and Oratory*. Chicago: Fairbanks & Palmer, 1884, [Pages 604-606 on RGI.] OU.

613 Whitney, James A. *A Word to the Orthodox in Re a Current Controversy*. [Between H. M. Field & Robert G. Ingersoll]. New York: Tibbal's Book Co., 1889, 18p. EBM.

614 Wilson, H. Clay. *A Tribute to Col. Robert G. Ingersoll*. Springfield, Illinois, n.p., 1907, 24p. NN.

615 [Woodruff, C. M.] *Another Letter to Mr. Ingersoll from a Believer*. Detroit: Author, 1888, 32p. DLC.

Appendix

Included below are titles which are known to have once existed, and which may still exist, but which the author was unable to identify or locate. Since the titles are not in the standard (i.e., Dresden Edition) form, proper placement of these titles within the body of this checklist was impossible.
They are included here for completeness.

A1 BREAKING THE FETTERS. Bristol, [England]: W. H. Morrish, [188?]. [TxU], [NN].

A2 CUBA. New York: Vincente, Mestore & Amabile, 1888. [DLC].

A3 INGERSOLL AT HOME. London: Freethought Publishing Co., [188?].

A4 INTERVIEW WITH INGERSOLL. London: Geo. Standring, 1884, 15p.

A5 MARRIAGE AND DIVORCE. London: Freethought Publishing Co., [189?].

A6 REFORM. [Brooklyn, N. Y.]: Brooklyn Philosophical Assoc., [n.d.?]

A7 RELIGION OF LOVE. Boston: J. H. West, 1912.

A8 SALVATION. London: Freethought Publishing Co., [188-].

ADDENDA

The item(s) below were discovered too late to be included either in the body of the checklist or in the index.

SECTION I

A9 AN ADDRESS TO THE COLORED PEOPLE (DE 9:5-17)

  a) [*Exit Magazine*, New York, 1969], 13L. [Pages numbered 5-17. Offset of DE.]

A10 ART AND MORALITY (DE 11:203-211)

  a) Progressive Publishing Co., London, 1890, 15p.
  b) R. Forder, London, [189-].

SECTION II

A11 Haldeman–Julius, E., ed. *Is Free Will a Fact or a Fallacy?* Girard, Kansas: Appeal to Reason, [c 1920], 56p. [Contains "Blasphemy," in part, and "Oration at a Child's Grave."]

SECTION VIC

A12 Bailey, Rev. G. S. *Ingersollism Exposed*, Ottumwa, Iowa: n.p., 1882, 8p.
OO.

A13 Burgess, Rev. William. *The Gladstone and Ingersoll Controversy*, Newayo, Michigan: The *Tribune* Job Printing Co., 188, 26p.
OO.

A14 Hawkins, Cyril. *Sketches, Including Scenes and Incidents of Distinguished "Buckeyes" and Others*, McConnelsville, Ohio: n.p., n.d., 62p. [RGI on pages 53-57.] OO.

A15 Moore, Rev. H. H. *The Anatomy of Atheism*, Cincinnati: Cranston & Stow, 1890, 365p. [An attempt to refute RGI specifically.]

A16 Simkins, W. W. *Criticisms on Ingersoll's Notions of the Gods and the Bible*, Pella, Iowa: Masteller & Co., 1876, 56p.

Index

113

120